NATIONAL COUNCIL FOR THE SOCIAL STUDIES

BULLETIN NO. 73

Community Study: Applications and Opportunities

MARK C. SCHUG AND R. BEERY, EDITORS

National Council for the Social Studies

President
Jean Craven
Albuquerque Public Schools
Albuquerque, New Mexico

President-Elect
Donald H. Bragaw
New York State Department of Education
Albany, New York

Vice President
Paul R. Shires
Glendale-Nicolet High School
Milwaukee, Wisconsin

Executive Director
Frances Haley
Washington, DC

Director of Publications
Charles R. Rivera
Washington, DC

Executive Secretary Emeritus
Merrill F. Hartshorn
Washington, DC

Board of Directors
Charlotte C. Anderson
James A. Banks
Janna Bremer
Phyllis Clarke
Ann Cotton
Lois W. Daniel
Betty S. Dean
Carole L. Hahn
Jean Hutt
Clair Keller
Bob Lynch
Mary McFarland
C. Frederick Risinger
John Rossi
Donald O. Schneider
Lois Conley Smith
Bob Stahl

Publications Board
Caroline Penn, *Chairperson*
Marlowe Berg
Margaret Carter
Shirla McClain
Thomas Turner
Denny Schillings
Linda Wojtan
Ex officito:
Paul R. Shires
Frances Haley
Charles R. Rivera
Boone C. Colegrove

Library of Congress Catalog Card Number 84-062025
ISBN 0-87986-048-0
Copyright© 1984 by the
NATIONAL COUNCIL FOR THE SOCIAL STUDIES
3501 Newark Street, NW, Washington, DC 20016

Table of Contents

ABOUT THE AUTHORS		**IV**
CHAPTER I	**R. BEERY AND MARK C. SCHUG** Young People and Community	**1**
CHAPTER II	**ROBERT WOYACH** Using the Local Community to Teach About the Global Community	**15**
CHAPTER III	**MARK C. SCHUG** Approaches for Teaching Community Economics	**29**
CHAPTER IV	**R. BEERY** State History and Community Study	**41**
CHAPTER V	**TERRY ZELLER** Using the Visual Arts to Interpret the Community	**57**
CHAPTER VI	**R. BEERY AND ROBERT J. TODD** Citizenship Grounded in Community	**75**
CHAPTER VII	**DIANE HEDIN** Developing Values Through Community Service	**92**
INDEX		**107**

About The Authors

R. Beery is Director of Curriculum and Instruction in the Rochester Public Schools, Rochester, Minnesota. He has directed numerous curriculum development projects with special emphasis on the local community. Beery has written student and teacher materials for the intermediate level, for junior high school, and for senior high school, in sociology, anthropology, history, ethnic studies, government, and current issues. He has published articles on community studies, economic education, and social studies goals in such journals as *Phi Delta Kappan, Social Education,* and *Social Studies.* He has taught in the inner city schools of Minneapolis and at the University of Minnesota.

Diane Hedin is an Associate Professor at the Center for Youth Development and Research, University of Minnesota, where she teaches courses in adolescent development, experiential education, and youth work for persons in formal and informal education. Hedin has directed community service and experiential learning programs in public schools, and has done a series of evaluations on the impact of youth participation and experiential learning on secondary students, including the first national study of such programs.

Mark C. Schug is an Associate Professor of Education at the University of Wisconsin — Milwaukee. He taught social studies for eight years in two public school districts. He currently teaches courses in social studies methods and economic education. His articles have appeared in such journals as *Phi Delta Kappan, Educational Leadership, Social Education, Theory and Research in Social Education,* and *Social Studies.* Schug has also prepared student and teacher materials for use at the middle school and high school levels in economics, history, government, and experiential education.

Robert J. Todd is the Social Studies Specialist in the Rochester Public Schools, Rochester, Minnesota. He has been an elementary teacher in Rochester and has served as project developer for the Minnesota Community Studies Project and the Citizenship Education Experiences Project of the Rochester Public Schools. Todd has also served as Managing Editor of *Minnesota Issues,* a newspaper for high school students. He has conducted numerous presentations at state and national social studies conferences.

Robert B. Woyach is a political scientist and Associate Director of the Citizenship Development and Global Perspectives Program of The Ohio State University's Mershon Center. Woyach has conducted research on the international relations of cities and on organizational factors affecting participation in local world affairs organizations. He has developed three sets of global perspectives curriculum materials for use in upper elementary, middle school, and high school classes. Two of these explicitly employ community resources to teach about global involvement and impact.

Terry Zeller is the Chairman of the Department of Education, Rochester Museum and Science Center, Rochester, New York. From 1979 to 1982 he was Coordinator of Adult Education at the Minneapolis Institute of Arts, and he has held faculty appointments at such institutions as Texas Tech University, the University of Arkansas, Western Michigan University, and the University of Nebraska. Zeller holds advanced degrees in history, education, and art history/museology.

CHAPTER I / R. BEERY AND MARK C. SCHUG

Young People and Community

The excitement, fears, and happiness of childhood, and the ecstasy, uncertainty, and embarrassments of adolescence are intense emotions, experienced within concrete community settings. These powerful feelings involve little of the subtlety and abstractness of the social sciences. At this level of simplicity and immediacy, intense daily interactions within the flow that is community have the greatest importance and meaning. Issues such as military policies, the basic structure of the international economy, and the changing quality of the world's resource base are vital to the survival of human life and deserve searching consideration in the social studies. But they are not the basic, felt concerns of the young.

Just one step removed from the vital personal preoccupations of youth are concerns about the quality and availability of local health care, patterns of employment and unemployment in the local area, the activities of the local power elite, and the adequacy of community services. These matters too have an immediate impact on daily life. They are also concerns that can be readily influenced by citizen participation within the local community's existing institutions.

But where is the local community treated in any depth in social studies? In the primary grades, teachers discuss community helpers, and there are other cursory references in the following years as the focus of the social studies program moves to the larger and seemingly more significant world. The local community is not a central organizing theme in the social studies program. The basic assumption underlying this Bulletin is that local community — the social settings our students are experiencing daily — needs to be a direct focus of the social studies at every level.

There are reasons why the local community is not a central focus in school programs. Community study requires more preparation by the teacher and student than other approaches to social studies. Texts are not there to be evaluated, adopted, purchased, and used to give structure and substance to lessons. When there is so much that can be taught from textbooks and other standard curricular materials; when students resist being pushed out of the classroom to dig up, organize, and create their own information; when a variety of special interest groups become alarmed if young people probe real issues of the day, a harried social studies teacher might well ask: *"Why bother?"*

Why Teachers Do Bother

Citizenship education involves knowledge and skills essential to functioning within economic, political, and socio-cultural systems. To be an effective member of society, an individual needs to learn how to make society responsive to legitimate personal and group needs, wants, and desires.

The position statement of the National Council for the Social Studies on the Essentials of the Social Studies begins with the assertion that "Citizen participation in public life is essential to the health of our democratic system," and it summarizes the ideal as "Social studies programs which combine the acquisition of knowledge and skills with an understanding of the application of democratic beliefs to life through practice at social participation...." The statement concludes with an emphasis on the need for "the will to take part in public affairs."

In order to become reality, this ideal must be integrated into the expanding experiences of the young, and a persistent element in their developing notions and feelings about self. How can social studies teachers accomplish this? The Essentials of the Social Studies states, "Connecting the classroom with the community provides many opportunities for students to learn the basic skills of participation, from observation to advocacy." All of the essential components of the social studies must be grounded in concrete realities that have meaning for young people — including those with minimal interest and capabilities. That is, the knowledge, beliefs, and skills basic to a solid social education for democratic citizenship require personal will and engagement which can be nurtured by focusing on the concrete contexts of family, school, and community. Without a consistent and recurrent focus on the personal and the local, it is doubtful whether the abstract ideals and concepts of citizenship education can be attained.

This Bulletin is not simply a series of suggestions for "utilizing" the community setting as good illustrative material for teaching the goals of the social studies. Focus on the local to enliven social science generalizations is, of course, a legitimate use of community, but it is secondary to systematic consideration of the processes of individual, family, and group life within local settings. Once time is given to careful and sensitive examinations of the personal experiences of students, then it is appropriate to move on to closely related concerns about family, neighborhood, and community and to consider their relationships with the state, region, nation, and world. But it is important that students redirect their attention to immediate experience as they are urged to focus on ever-expanding horizons.

Youngsters at all ages are engaged in learning from rich and varied community experiences. Indeed, the most important learning occurs in "natural" community settings. The beginning kindergartner has already learned the need for give and take in play "communities." Children and youth are a vital part of the consumer economy. The high percentage of young people engaged in part-time employment has major implications for their understanding of and attitudes toward business. Many young people's jobs are key elements in their dynamic conceptions of self.

While much of the content of existing social studies ignores the vital self/social concerns of the young, it also violates our knowledge of developmental capabilities. Teachers tend to teach above the level of many students when they deal in abstractions such as supply and demand, social contract, and cultural lag. Frequently, we assume too rich a base of experience and too high a cognitive level on the part of our students. There is ample evidence that most high school students in the United States do not engage in formal reasoning. The predictable result is that young people often learn social studies concepts in a superficial fashion. They memorize definitions of culture, role, and federalism. They try to recall the capitals of the states and the names of cabinet members. They fail to get much farther in terms of basic comprehension and analysis of problems.

In a review of learning theory, Shepardson and Schug (1982) suggest that we need to present students at all grade levels with a broader range of firsthand social experiences. Students should have a chance to manipulate and interact with the environment. In the elementary and junior high schools, special emphasis should be placed upon concepts which have concrete, observable referents which can be experienced directly. Community study provides the type of concrete, firsthand experiences which are appropriate to students' developmental levels.

Motivation is another key variable in student learning. A number of indicators suggest that student motivation in social studies is not high. The lack of variety in teaching social studies tends to reduce student participation. Textbooks, the most commonly used teaching tool, still tend to emphasize highly factual information and to avoid touching upon sensitive or controversial issues. Several studies have documented the fact that most students do not feel that social studies is meaningful to their lives. Morrissett et al. (1980), for example, found that students view social studies as less useful and less important to their needs than English or mathematics. Another study (Schug et al., 1984) concluded that:

- English, mathematics, and reading rank higher than social studies, because students see these subjects as preparing them for future careers and teaching important skills they will need in the future.
- Students identify social studies as neither a favorite nor a least favorite course. It may be that students are simply indifferent to social studies.
- Students view other courses in the curriculum as providing greater opportunities for active learning.

One way to improve student interest in social studies may be to strengthen community study as a component of the curriculum. Community study can provide a view of social processes and social institutions at close range which can help to increase the motivation of students.

History teachers sometimes complain that it is difficult for students to grasp the concepts which they are trying to teach. Filmstrips and movies help, as do reading firsthand accounts and case studies and playing simulation games. Community study can help by involving students in the creation of real experiences in the local community. Students who conduct oral history interviews with local senior citizens or do volunteer work cataloging materials at a county historical society are developing a clearer understanding of the real meaning of history than those students who merely read and discuss textbook accounts.

In many ways, the local community serves as a microcosm of the broader society. To state the obvious, communities are basic components of society. Local communities are interdependent systems which can provide concrete illustrations of social functions. Local governments at one time were nearly self-sufficient operations, levying local taxes and providing local services. Today, local government and other levels of government are much more interdependent. The traditional three tiers of local, state, and federal government have given way to a marbled structure wherein all layers of government depend upon and interact with one another. The same thing has happened in the economy. Many local or regional firms have undergone dramatic expansion and now serve national and international markets. Many local communities have businesses which operate on a global scale. Growth of the regulatory role of the federal government has also expanded federal influence to many firms and other economic organizations. One result of these changes is that local communities can be rich sources of data about complex social concerns.

Identifying the local community as a microcosm is an accurate and useful insight, but it is also inadequate, if not condescending. As John Naisbitt convincingly argues in *Megatrends* (1982), three of the "Ten New Directions Transforming Our Lives" are decentralization, self-help, and participatory democracy — all of which focus on intense involvement in the immediate community. From this perspective, the local community is more than a reflection of broader social systems.

Moreover, Naisbitt cites evidence of increased action by local governments, imaginatively responding to a range of issues affecting the quality of life. Also, he contends that entrepreneurship is alive and flourishing as never before within dynamic communities across the land.

Community study in the schools may be a first step to stimulating interest and reducing negative attitudes. It may provide the first opportunity for young people to become engaged in public life and learn essential participation skills.

Studying local history, interviewing members of the city council, performing volunteer community services, and joining advocacy groups in the local community are all ways in which young people can gain experience as responsible participants.

A final, urgent reason why social studies teachers should work more closely with their local communities is to rebuild the relationship between the school and the community which has deteriorated seriously in recent years. Social studies is one area in the curriculum which has great potential for community involvement. Mehlinger (1981) notes that education once operated under a consensus model of politics which has steadily yielded to a conflict model. Legislation for minimum competency tests for teachers and students, defeats of school referenda, teacher strikes, and controversies over textbook selection are all evidence of increased distrust between the community and the school.

There are no easy ways of reducing distrust and improving understanding between school and community. However, integrating community study experiences into the social studies curriculum is one way to begin. Community study enables teachers and community members to interact with each other, sharing the common goal of improving the educational experiences of the community's youth. For example, inviting a local banker to speak to an economics class can have obvious educational benefits for the students. Consider the other benefits of the experience: The banker feels proud to be asked to contribute to the school program, the teacher and the banker communicate directly in setting up the details of the talk, the teacher appreciates the important contributions that community resource people can make to learning, and the banker learns what a day in the life of a teacher is like. Even the rather common practice of using guest speakers can help to move teachers, students, and community members toward mutual understanding.

It is time that social studies programs play a more deliberate role in facilitating these natural learning processes. Community study is more than field trips and guest speakers. It involves an imaginative, sensitive awareness of the immediate concerns of the young. It requires selection and relies upon the use of a variety of lively activities to explore felt and known realities in new ways, and to connect new insights with past experience. It is the honest use of content from life. It is also a focus for new forms of cooperation between the school and the community.

Social Studies Content

Figure 1 shows four dimensions of community study. One dimension of community study is content. Social studies programs seldom use the local setting extensively as a source of content. Rarely does the social studies curriculum provide a direct opportunity for students to study their own community. Elementary social studies programs usually have units on the neighborhood and the community at grades two and three. Unfortunately, teachers tend to use commercially available materials which teach about community in a general way or focus on case studies about life in specific communities such as Chicago, San Francisco, Moscow, or Brasilia. The same is true at the secondary level. Teachers periodically bring in local examples to illustrate points being made in government, economics, geography, or history courses, but generally the curriculum makes no provision for a systematic study of the local community.

Using the community as a source of content does have some disadvantages. Standard curricular materials about local communities are often not available. School districts usually need to develop their own local materials. Developing curricular materials usually means releasing teachers from regular teaching assignments or organizing summer projects to prepare units, design materials, identify field trip sites, and make contacts with potential guest speakers. Ideally, all teachers who will ultimately teach the activities should be involved in the development process. In addition, inservice training will probably be necessary if teachers are to use the activities effectively. This adds up to a substantial commitment on the part of the local school district. However, many school districts have allocated sufficient resources to develop materials and activities

Content
local history
local geography
community economy
family history
local government
community issues

Skills
data-gathering
intellectual skills
decision-making
interpersonal skills
participation skills

Democractic Practices and Beliefs

Service
internships
service projects

Learning Experiences
guest speakers
field trips
tutors
interviews

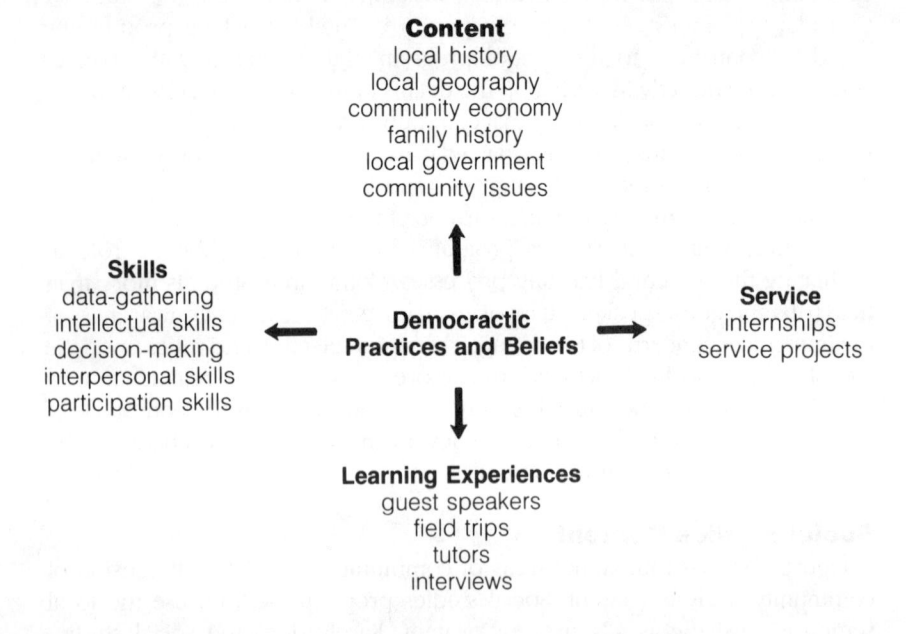

Figure 1. Dimensions of Local Community Study in a Social Studies Program

for local study. Their success and enthusiasm suggest that community curriculum development projects are worthwhile.

The local community can provide rich examples to illustrate many concepts and generalizations from the social sciences. History, economics, political science, and geography are areas of study easily adapted to community study. Courses in citizenship, law, values, future studies, and global studies can often take advantage of local community content to illustrate important ideas. The following is a list of sample units which can be developed using the local community as content.

- Neighborhood and Community History
- Law in the Community
- Community Economics
- Local Government
- The Community and the World
- Economic Community Case Studies
- The Community in the Future

Learning Experiences

Another dimension of community study represented in Figure 1 is learning activities. Using the local community as a source of learning activities is the most widely recognized aspect of community study. Field trips and guest speakers are the most common elements of community-based learning experiences. Figure 2 presents a "starter list" of possible community field trip sites and resource persons.

Field Trip Sites
Local historical society
Public museum
Pioneer cemetery
School board meeting
City council meeting
Public hearing
Political party headquarters
Manufacturers
Banks
Neighborhoods
Courthouse
Human service agencies
Treatment center for the mentally retarded or the mentally ill
Historical Sites

Guest Speakers
Public Officials: Mayor, city council member, legislator, congressional representative, school board member, county board member
Business People: Banker, stockbroker, real estate salesperson, manufacturer, student employer.
Labor Leaders: Union member, local officer.
Civic Groups: League of Women Voters, American Bar Association, Chamber of Commerce.
Public Employees: Social worker, employment counselor, urban planner, police officer, fire fighter, family counselor, probation officer.

Figure 2. Community Learning Experiences

Field trips can provide optimal learning experiences in social studies. A morning spent collecting data at an old cemetery or taking a walking tour through an ethnic neighborhood can be a worthwhile learning experience which builds student enthusiasm for history. Some precautions need to be taken, however, if the trip is to be successful. Students need to be prepared before the trip, so that they know what to look for and how the field experience ties in with past learning. In addition, the teacher needs to provide a thoughtful follow-up, so that students can reflect on what they did and saw.

There are a variety of ways in which community resource people can be used in social studies. The most frequent approach is to contact individuals to be guest speakers. The format that the teacher uses for the guest speaker will vary with the topic, the speaker, and the grade-level of the students. The following alternative formats might be considered:

- Press Conference: Speaker opens with a *brief* introductory statement and then takes questions from the group.
- Student Questions: Class provides written questions for the speaker which he or she can respond to in the presentation.
- Guest Lecturer: Speaker should break frequently for questions, bring visuals, and use dramatic and well-thought-out examples.

Another way of using community resource people is to assign students individually or in pairs to conduct interviews and to share their information with other class members. For example, elementary students have been successful at interviewing grandparents or senior citizens in their neighborhoods about what life was like during the 1930s.

The technique of using community resource people as volunteers should not be overlooked. Frequently, students at upper grade levels, college students, parents, and senior citizens are willing to perform volunteer work as social studies tutors. Using volunteer tutors provides a useful instructional aid which can help individualize instruction and bring more variety to teaching.

Service

Community service is a third deminsion of community study. Judge Mary Conway Kohler had community service in mind when she wrote: "Maturity is measured by one's ability to accept and follow through on responsibilities for one's self, one's family, one's work, and one's community. To make the transition to adulthood, young people urgently need opportunities to be responsible, caring, participating members of our society" (1981, p. 426).

More recently, the Carnegie Foundation for the Advancement of Teaching highlighted this need when it identified as one of "four essential goals" of a high school education the involvement of all students in activities that "fulfill their social and civic obligations through school and community service" (Boyer, 1983, p. 67). In its "Agenda for Action," the foundation noted that the young "should be given opportunities to reach beyond themselves and feel more responsibly engaged" (p. 306).

A community study program is not balanced unless it provides opportunities for young people to perform volunteer service to the local community. Community service provides students with real and meaningful experiences that are without parallel in the social studies classroom. One way to incorporate community service into the social studies program is to arrange specific, short-term service projects which can be readily performed by the students. The following are some examples of such activities:
- Organizing a recycling project
- Organizing a clean-up campaign at school or in the neighborhood
- Assisting in neighborhood energy "audits"
- Participating in voter registration campaigns
- Supporting voter information programs
- Performing volunteer work for a political party or candidate
- Performing volunteer work at a museum or historical society
- Visiting nursing homes or rehabilitation centers for the retarded or mentally ill
- Participating in marathons to raise money for community service organizations
- Collecting oral histories
- Conducting opinion polls about local issues

The concept of community service can be significantly extended by giving students an opportunity for long-term participation in the community. Often, students receive social studies credit for doing volunteer community service over a quarter, trimester, or semester. Students are usually released for a specific time each day to travel to a community site to perform specific tasks. Day-care centers, elementary schools, tutoring programs, nursing homes, senior citizen centers, sheltered workshops, state hospitals, legal aid programs, and peer counseling programs are just a few of the types of community agencies which often use young volunteers on an extended basis. Many such programs have been in operation for years in various parts of the nation. A recently completed national study found that community service programs are powerful tools for promoting personal and intellectual development and can be more effective than classroom instruction (Conrad and Hedin, 1982).

The notion of community service need not stop with students. Social studies teachers themselves may assume active roles in the local community. Social studies teachers who serve on community boards, hold public office, or perform other types of volunteer service quickly develop a thorough understanding of local government, the community economy, and local issues. Social studies teachers who perform community service are also an important model of responsible citizen participation. Finally, the teacher's participation in the community can help to reduce distrust between school and community.

Skills

The fourth dimension of community study represented in Figure 1 is skill development. The Essentials of the Social Studies treats thinking skills as the tools with which individuals relate knowledge to beliefs and purposeful action.

Data-gathering Skills. Learning to:
Acquire information by observation
Locate information from a variety of sources
Compile, organize, and evaluate information
Extract and interpret information
Communicate orally and in writing

Intellectual Skills. Learning to:
Compare things, ideas, events, and situations on the basis of similarities and differences
Classify or group items in categories
Ask appropriate and searching questions
Draw conclusions or inferences from evidence
Arrive at general ideas
Make sensible predictions from generalizations

Decision-making Skills. Learning to:
Consider alternative solutions
Consider the consequences of each solution
Make decisions and justify them in relationship to democratic principles
Act, based on those decisions

Interpersonal Skills. Learning to:
See things from the point of view of others
Understand one's beliefs, feelings, abilities, and shortcomings and how they affect relations with others
Use group generalizations without stereotyping or arbitrarily classifying individuals
Recognize value in individuals different from oneself and groups different from one's own
Work effectively with others as a group member
Give and receive constructive criticism
Accept responsibility and respect the rights and property of others

Participation Skills. Learning to:
Work effectively in groups — organizing, planning, making decisions, taking action
Form coalitions of interest with other groups
Persuade, compromise, bargain
Practice patience and perseverance in working for one's goal
Develop experience in cross-cultural situations

[Source: *Essentials of the Social Studies* (Washington, DC: National Council for the Social Studies, n.d.)]

Figure 3. Skills for Community Study

The statement further describes thinking skills as "those skills which help assure rational behavior in social settings." Participation skills are required in "connecting the classroom with the community." Figure 3 presents those thinking and participation skills identified in the Essentials statement.

Deliberate attention to development and consistent use of these skills in community study emphasizes the kinds of inquiry which this study involves. Questions are the heart of community study, and they are frequently questions whose answers are not readily available in print or known by the teacher or a local official. Indeed, answers often lead to new, important, but unanswered, questions. Here, the skills develop naturally, and their importance is clear.

Democratic Beliefs and Practices

The Essentials of the Social Studies stresses the need to focus on "the basic principles of our democratic constitutional order," as they are embodied in such practices as due process, equal protection, and civic participation. These practices and beliefs are viewed as rooted in the concepts of justice, equality, responsibility, freedom, diversity, and privacy.

When these principles are violated, it is usually at the local level — vigilante justice, violence in response to court-ordered busing, and, more subtly, those local pressures that cause self-censorship because of the lack of respect for diversity of belief and opinion.

When the social studies program focuses attention on knowledge, critical thinking and participation skills, and service experiences within the local community, these democratic principles will become clear and strong, with greater likelihood of transfer beyond structured classroom experiences.

The actualization of the society's democratic potential depends upon rational and principled action grounded in a commitment to the rights of others and a dedication to one's own responsibilities within the community.

Planning

The most widely overlooked and fundamental aspect of community study is involvement of the community in the planning of the curriculum. Fantini (1980) points out that public education in the United States was never intended to become a completely professional matter. Yet, educators are often reluctant to invite public participation in curriculum planning. There are, however, many sound reasons why the community should be systematically involved. Fantini cites a study by Wegenaar (1977) which presents evidence that schools with high levels of community participation have higher levels of student achievement than schools with lower levels of community involvement and support. Involving the community in planning the social studies program can also help teachers discover new teaching resources in the community, such as guest speakers, field trip sites, and organizations that welcome student volunteers to participate in their programs. Community participation can also help teachers handle controversial issues, deal with censorship questions, and gain an awareness of community expectations.

There are several ways for social studies educators to involve the community in curriculum planning. One common technique is to establish a social studies advisory committee. Advisory committees have several inherent advantages. They provide a form of direct, face-to-face communication which can stimulate creative suggestions for improving programs and resolving problems. They can help foster mutual understanding among the participants. Classroom teachers are exposed to the worries and concerns of community members, while community representatives become aware of the perspectives and concerns of teachers. In addition, advisory committees are inexpensive and relatively easy to set up and administer.

Establishing a social studies advisory committee does, however, have some drawbacks. These groups can become more than advisory. Members may be disappointed if their suggestions are not incorporated into the curriculum, or if they feel they are merely "window dressing" in someone's public relations effort. Nonetheless, experience with a wide variety of advisory groups strongly suggests that the benefits of such an approach clearly outweigh the potential problems.

Certainly, there are other ways to elicit community participation in program planning. Social studies educators can conduct periodic surveys of parents and community groups. Social studies teachers can be encouraged to serve on community boards and be active in community organizations. Community representatives can be appointed to serve on existing social studies curriculum and textbook selection committees. The point is that some formal means should be devised which consistently involves community members with teachers in planning and reviewing the social studies program.

Limits

Drawing upon community, family, and self as rich sources of knowledge and information can promote discovery of key concepts. These resources can also be used to apply and test out given generalizations. The danger in either case is the assumption that data from local events "prove" something broader about the economic, political, or social behavior of people in the state, region, nation, or world. Students must be taught to delimit their conclusions carefully and to summarize their findings within the boundaries of their explorations.

This need to define the limits of personal and local data may, on the other hand, be one of the values of using personal and community sources and settings. Too often, individuals generalize about others from their own narrow experiences. Ethnic biases bolstered by an encounter with a few of "them," indignant outrage based on a widely publicized case of welfare fraud, disgust aroused by one dishonest politician are examples or generalized responses which need to be addressed as social studies programs teach thinking skills.

In Conclusion

This chapter has presented several reasons why community study should be a fundamental part of the social studies program. It has emphasized that community study affords an opportunity for dealing with self and society within the immediate context in which students live. It provides accessible content for developing and using abstract social studies concepts. It can guide development of specific thinking and participation skills, as well as improve student motivation in social studies. Community study contributes to the growth of reasoned commitment to democratic principles and practices and involves students in the first level of participation in public life. Finally, it can help to reduce distrust between the community and the school.

Community study involves using the community as a source of social studies content in the curriculum; using the community as a source of learning activities; engaging students and social studies teachers in volunteer community service; and teaching and reinforcing important skills through participation in the community. A balanced K–12 social studies program is one which makes use of opportunities for students and the community to interact in each of these ways, and which highlights community participation in planning the social studies program.

The material that follows in this Bulletin deals with selected notions and activities for developing some of the dimensions of community study introduced in this chapter. Each chapter explores community study in relation to specific content areas in the social studies — global studies, economics, state history, the arts, citizenship, and valuing.

There are, of course, other valuable areas of community study that are not considered here. Geography is one such area. Skills and concepts derived from community study can be used to guide students in discovering, exploring, and manipulating their environments. Mapping activities can make a variety of skills immediately applicable. Directly observable places, events, and processes can be related to statistical data in readily understandable ways. Statistics regarding climate and changing land use patterns invite classroom use.

Use of artifacts is suggested in some of the chapters; however, the whole field of archaeology has a variety of applications which are not treated here. James Deetz (1978) asserts that "artifacts reflect cognitions. Material culture systems represent the minds of the people who put them together .... No one was carrying any ideological grudge when he threw the garbage out the door. When we dig up that garbage it informs us unintentionally. It is probably the most bias-free evidence we have." Garbage, especially that which has not yet been buried — today's leavings — can tell a great deal about local society and illuminate key community issues of genuine importance.

Another aspect of community study not considered here is the psychology of peer-group processes. The sociology of local power structures could also be a focus of community study, but it is not treated here.

However compulsive we may sometimes be about classifying knowledge and information by disciplines, community study is naturally integrative. And that is a key virtue: community study invites the young to focus naturally on realities, avoiding curricular segmentation that is often meaningless.

Many other aspects of community study invite attention in social studies. It is our hope that this NCSS Bulletin will begin the process for teachers and students.

Bibliography

Boyer, E. L. *High School: A Report on Secondary Education in America*. New York: Harper and Row, 1983.

Conrad, D., and Hedin, D. *Executive Summary of the Final Report of the Experiential Education Evaluation Project*. Center for Youth Development and Research, University of Minnesota, 1982.

Conrad, D., Hedin, D., and Simon, P. *Minnesota Youth Poll: Youth's Views on Politics and Public Issues*. Center for Youth Development and Research, Miscellaneous Report 178, Agricultural Experiment Station, University of Minnesota, 1981.

Deetz, J. "Material Culture," in Botein et al. (eds.) *Experiments in History Teaching*, Cambridge, MA: Harvard-Danforth Center for Teaching and Learning, 1977, 17.

Fantini, M.D. "Community Participation: Alternative Patterns and Their Consequence on Educational Achievement," Paper presented at the American Educational Research Association, Spring 1980.

Kohler, M.C. "Developing Responsible Youth Through Youth Participation." *Phi Delta Kappan,* February 1981, 426–428.

Mehlinger, H. D. "Social Studies: Some Goals and Priorities, "*The Social Studies: Eightieth Yearbook of the National Society for the Study of Education*. H. D. Mehlinger, and O. L. Davies, Jr. (eds.) Chicago: University of Chicago Press, 1981 244–269.

Morrissett, I., Hawke, S., and Superka, D. P. "Six Problems for Social Studies in the 1980's." *Social Education,* November/December 1980, 501–569.

Naisbitt, J. *Megatrends: Ten New Directions Transforming Our Lives*. New York: Warner Books, 1982.

Schug, M. C., Improving Teacher Education by Using Program Advisory Committees," *Social Studies,* July/August 1982, 148–150.

Schug, M. C., Todd, R. J., and Beery, R. W. "Why Kids Don't Like Social Studies," *Social Education,* May 1984, 382–384.

Shepardson, R. D., and Schug, M. C., *A Review of Cognitive Development Theory As It Relates to Economic Education*. New York: Joint Council on Economic Education, 1982.

Wagenaar, T. C. "School Achievement Level Vis-à-vis Community Involvement and Support." Paper presented at the American Sociological Association, Chicago, 1977.

CHAPTER II / ROBERT B. WOYACH

Using the Local Community to Teach About the Global Community

The world has changed dramatically in the last fifty years. During this time, our perceptions of the world have changed as well. Once scholars, politicians, and others saw "the world" simply as a set of "countries." These countries vied with one another for power. They maneuvered for influence, and attempted to survive and prosper in a world that could be quite inhospitable.

Today, "the world" appears to be much more complicated.[1] For one thing, the cast of characters has grown. The number of independent countries has more than tripled in the past fifty years. New types of actors, including multinational corporations, religious movements, foundations, and revolutionary groups, have come on stage. The concerns of the world community have also multiplied. Questions of peace and war continue to be central issues, but heads of state also discuss inflation, recession, and job security at summit meetings. Farmers in Kansas and Australia carefully follow the news about Soviet grain harvests. California environmental groups protest the killing of whales by Soviet and Japanese fishermen. State legislatures in Connecticut and Wisconsin debate whether state monies should be invested in corporations doing business in South Africa because of its apartheid laws.

Underlying these increasingly complex considerations is a critical change in "the world." Today, as never before, world affairs have become a part of the everyday lives of ordinary people.[2] Events and issues on the other side of the world now affect the quality of life from Portland to Poughkeepsie. From Miami to Moline, consumers, businesspeople, local politicians, and organization leaders now make decisions that have international implications.

The diffusion of international causes and effects poses a challenge and an opportunity for the curriculum. Students need to develop competencies, skills, attitudes, and knowledge which previous generations did not need. Teachers should portray the world as it touches the lives of students, not as something distant and exotic. Similarly, the students' daily experiences and their community become potential resources for understanding and learning about the world.

---

[1]See Lee Anderson, *Schooling and Citizenship in a Global Age: Explorations into the Meaning and Significance of Global Education* (Bloomington, IN: Social Studies Development Center, 1979).

[2]See Chadwick Alger, "A World of Cities, or Good Foreign Policies Begin at Home" (Columbus, OH: Mershon Center, 1976).

The Changing Agenda of International Education

A number of educators have attempted to articulate educational goals and objectives which can serve as guidelines for preparing students to participate in this changing world.[3] These goals and objectives differ in many respects. Nevertheless, two ideas are at the heart of them all. The first is that the world has become interdependent. This concept sums up the changes that have occurred in the world in this century. Global systems of activity have expanded. As a result, the rest of the world affects us and we affect it. What were once local and regional issues have become international concerns. In certain respects, all of the people on the planet now share a common future. Thus, if we hope to preserve our democratic traditions, Americans must be capable of exercising citizenship with respect to international as well as national, state, and local issues.

The second idea that constantly appears in global education guidelines is that interdependence forces people together — for better or for worse — whether they are prepared or not. Increasingly, Americans must deal directly with people from different cultures. All citizens must confront issues whose global scope requires that people from different countries cooperate. In such a world, students must understand that people from varying backgrounds will perceive and evaluate the world around them differently. Students need to learn to deal with these differences. They must be able to identify what is valuable and valid in the cultures and perspectives of others. This is possible only if students appreciate the fact that despite their differences, people around the world have similar needs and basically similar responses to those needs.

The Dimensions and Variety of Community Resources

Most local communities provide a rich environment for teaching about the world. But identifying the available resources can often be difficult. Precisely because world affairs have become part of everyday life, international resources may not always seem "international."

Basically, the resources available in a community are of three types:
- **People,** including experts on world affairs and individuals who participate in international activities of all sorts.
- **Organizations,** including business firms, universities, voluntary groups, and civic institutions which engage in international activities or provide services to those who do.
- **Activities** of local organizations and people which link the community to people in other parts of the world.

The following social map of a medium-sized midwestern city[4] can make these categories more explicit.

---

[3]See, for example, Lee Anderson, op. cit., James M. Becker, "The World and the School: A Case for World-Centered Education," in James M. Becker, editor, *Schooling for a Global Age* (New York: (McGraw-Hill, 1979), and Robert G. Hanvey, "An Attainable Global Perspective" (New York: Global Perspectives in Education, 1976).

[4]From Robert B. Woyach, "Working on Methods of Inventorying Community Linkages" (Columbus, OH: Mershon Center, July 1974).

A SOCIAL MAP OF THE INTERNATIONAL CONNECTIONS OF COLUMBUS OHIO

Sectors and Examples of Organizations
I. Economic
   A. Manufacturing
   B. Trade (consumers, exporters, importers, transport companies, groceries, department stores)
   C. Service (banks, insurance companies, law offices, research firms, hospitals, travel agencies)
   D. Agriculture/Mining
   E. Business, Professional and Labor Organizations (Chamber of Commerce, unions, business and professional women's organizations)

Key International Dimensions/Activities
exporting
importing
investing abroad
foreign investment locally
foreign personnel
travel
communication by telephone, mail, telegram, telex

II. Education
   A. Elementary and Secondary (schools; teachers groups; youth organizations — Boy Scouts and Girl Scouts; exchange groups — AFS, YFU)
   B. Post-secondary (colleges and universities, adult education programs, foreign student clubs)

student/teacher exchanges
foreign students
travel
curriculum, programs
equipment/materials made abroad

III. Religious (churches, synagogues, denominational offices, interdenominational groups)

travel
communication
donations abroad
missionaries
study programs

IV. Recreation/Cultural
   A. Arts (museums, theaters, folk-art groups, performing art companies)
   B. Ethnic Groups/Restorations
   C. Sports (teams, athletic groups)
   D. Other (zoo, historical museums, libraries, ham radio operators)

travel
instruments, works of art, animals, equipment, music, dances, movies, books
communication

V. Mass Media (newspapers, magazines, television, radio)

news from abroad
news about international activity reported locally
travel

VI. Civic/Governmental
   A. Civic Groups (League of Women Voters, fraternal groups, service organizations, world affairs council, aid organizations)
   B. Government (local, county, state, federal officers, voters, foreign consultates)
   C. Military

travel, live abroad
send money abroad
educational programs, political programs
bills, lobbying efforts on international issues
communication

This social map demonstrates the extent to which international affairs have become woven into the fabric of a community. In Columbus, Ohio, world affairs "experts" are no longer a specialized elite. People with specialized international roles — e.g., export managers, international relations professors — can be found in virtually every sector of community life. Likewise, many other people who are not involved in specialized international roles also routinely engage in international activities. In fact, the list of people with significant international links includes consumers and voters, even though these groups may pay little attention to the international impact of their decisions and actions.

Strategies for Using the Community in Instruction

A wide array of international resources, embracing activities, people, and organizations, exists within virtually every community. Nonetheless, these resources may not always be readily available to teachers, and it is not always obvious how they can best be used to achieve instructional objectives.

Activities: The numerous activities connecting the local community and the world provide a starting point for teaching students about interdependence within the global community.

Elementary and secondary students can best be introduced to the extensive web of global systems through observations of their own and their families' daily international ties. A number of strategies can be used to sensitize students to the ways in which the world touches their lives.

For example:

Using the "Inventory of International Linkages," teachers can have students prepare lists of products and other activities which link them to the world. The lists can be used to map the class's linkages, showing with which regions it is most involved. Students might suggest reasons for differing levels of involvement as an introduction to the study of world geography.

INVENTORY OF INTERNATIONAL LINKAGES

Directions: List the types of *international contacts* you have had (e.g., imported products, people from other countries, trips abroad, news stories, stores) and the *countries or regions* with which you have had contact. Use two columns as follows:

| Type of Contact | Country or Region |

Use the following questions as a guide for completing the inventory:
1. From what countries or regions did your ancestors come?
2. What items from other countries are now on your person?
3. What items from other countries are in the classroom (other than those on your person)?
4. Have you or other members of your family been in contact with people from other countries in the past several weeks (e.g.,

LOCAL COMMUNITY/GLOBAL COMMUNITY

Type of Contact	Country or Region

through letters, in person, by telephone)?
5. What kind of international contacts have you or members of your family had through the media — e.g., newspapers, magazines, radio, television — in the past week?
6. Have you or other members of your family traveled abroad in the past several years? Where?
7. Check the kitchen, closets, basement and garage in your home. What other types of products from other countries are used by your family?
8. Look through the Yellow Pages of the telephone directory. What kinds of international contacts can you find there (e.g., restaurants, stores, importers, exporters, foreign consulates)?
9. Can you think of other international contacts you have had in the past 24 hours?

Inventory activities such as these can be introduced or followed up with readings which reinforce points made by students' inventories. "A Day in the Life of Seymour Someday,"[5] a reading particularly appropriate for world geography, outlines a typical day in the life of an American middle-school student. It then shows the incredible variety of ways in which Seymour participates in the activities of multinational corporations, systems of global transportation and communication, the international youth culture, shared symbols, and even ecological systems.

The following passage is from "An Englightened Day in the Life of Seymour Someday":

A DAY IN THE LIFE OF SEYMOUR SOMEDAY

I awoke at 7:00 a.m. to the ringing of my alarm clock.

Stop: You have encountered the international. Your clock is a product of the Sony Corporation, a Japanese-based multinational corporation. The clock was assembled in a Sony plant in Brazil from components produced in Japan, Mexico, and Germany. It was shipped to the United States in a Greek-owned ship manufactured in Sweden, licensed in Liberia, and staffed by a Portuguese crew.

Slowly, I showered and dressed, putting on my favorite pair of jeans.

Stop: Now you are wearing the international. Your shorts were made in Japan from cotton exported to Japan from the United States. Your socks were made in Taiwan using wool grown in Australia. The shirt that you are wearing was purchased at Montgomery Ward's, a subsidiary of Mobil Oil, one of the world's largest multinational businesses. The pair of jeans you like to wear were made by Levi Strauss, the biggest jean producer in the world. By putting on a pair of jeans you are participating in an international pop culture of young people throughout the world. . . .

---

[5]From Robert B. Woyach, *World Regions: The Local Connection*. This set of 53 lessons and activities is available from the Columbus Council on World Affairs, 50 W. Broad Street, Suite 3220, Columbus, OH 43215.

Another reading, "100% American," by Ralph Linton,[6] is particularly appropriate for American, state, local, and world history. This widely available article outlines the global origins of such everyday activities in American life as wearing pajamas and brushing teeth.

These types of readings are particularly useful in calling attention to international links which are hidden in indirect imports and historical borrowing.

The news media and other information sources within the community can also be used to show students the global involvement of their community. For example, teachers can:

- Have students prepare logs of international news stories by clipping items from local newspapers or writing abstracts of stories from television or radio. Stories which involve local people and organizations can be used in a bulletin board display which maps and profiles the community's international involvement.

- Have students use information from their media logs to prepare "news broadcasts" and "newspapers" of their own. The experience can reinforce writing and communication skills. It will also provide the basis for discussing the criteria editors use to choose news stories and how the media's space and time limitations affect our view of the world.

- Have students use the Yellow Pages of the telephone directory to identify categories of businesses which have ethnic and global connections. Students can identify visual clues in advertisements which show that an activity or business is international.

- Have students use cookbooks or recipes from home to identify the ethnic origins of dishes or the geographical origins of spices commonly used in their homes. An excellent resource for identifying the ethnic origins of dishes is the *American Heritage Cookbook (New York Times)*. Most encyclopedias will provide information on the origins of spices.

Inventory activities such as these can be used for critical thinking exercises designed to identify the impact of international linkages. Exercises which explicitly explore the impact of the world of the students' lives and futures can also be designed around specific local and personal connections. For example, teachers can:

- Have students identify products they use every day whose price has increased as a result of OPEC pricing decisions. These include records (all plastic products) and many chemicals, as well as gasoline and fuel oil.
- Use the worksheet "The Cost of Oil and You" to take a hypothetical look into the future. The worksheet asks students to make decisions about the type of car they would like to buy and where in the community they would like to live. Students then calculate the cost of commuting to work depending on these decisions and differing prices of gasoline. They then discuss how decisions made abroad might affect their future life styles, or at least the options open to them.
- Have students skim local newspapers for articles describing decisions or activities abroad which may affect their lives. They should be able to describe the decision and discuss or speculate on how it will affect people in the community.

---

[6]Originally published in *The American Mercury*, Vol. 40 (1937), pp. 427–429. The reading has been reproduced in various sources, including Chadwick Alger and David Hoovler, *You and Your Community in the World*. Learning Packages in International Studies. This learning package is available from the Consortium for International Studies Education, 199 W. 10th Avenue, Columbus, OH 43201.

THE COST OF OIL AND YOU

Answer questions 1 and 2. There are no right or wrong answers.

1. Which of the three types of cars listed below would you most like to own? (You must choose one of these three.)
   a. Cadillac Coupe de Ville (a large luxury car).
   b. Pontiac Firebird (a sporty car with high performance).
   c. Honda Civic (a small car).

2. Where would you most like to live when you have your own home or apartment? (Assume you work in the middle of a large city like Philadelphia, Birmingham, or Denver.)
   a. Within the city, near work.
   b. In the newer suburban areas, farther away from work.
   c. In rural areas, very far from work.

The following are real or hypothetical facts you will need to answer question 3.

Average Gasoline Prices
a. 1970—$ .30/gal
b. 1980—$ 1.20/gal
c. 2000—$10.00/gal (hypothetical)

1980 MPG Estimates
a. Cadillac: 18 miles per gallon
b. Pontiac: 22 miles per gallon
c. Honda: 41 miles per gallon

Average Annual Mileage Driving to and from Work from Various Residential Areas
a. Within the city: 2,400 miles
b. In the surrounding suburbs: 4,800 miles
c. In the rural area around the city: 7,200 miles

3. Using the above information, calculate the following:
   a. If you choose to buy a 1980 Pontiac Firebird and live in the suburbs, how much will it cost to drive to work during each of the following years?
      1970_____ 1980_____ 2000_____
   b. If gasoline costs $10/gallon in the year 2000, how much would it cost to drive the different cars?
      Firebird _____ Cadillac _____ Honda _____
      [from 3(a)]
   c. How much would it cost to drive the Firebird to work annually if you lived in the city or in rural areas rather than the suburbs?
      Suburbs _____ City _____ Rural Areas _____
      [from 3(a)]

4. Looking at the figures and your answers to questions 1 and 2, do you think changes in the price of gasoline might affect your choices about what car to buy and where to live? Why or why not?

In discussing the impact of world affairs on the community, it is important to note that all people will not be affected in the same way. For example, the increases in oil prices in the past decade have encouraged most Americans to adopt new life styles. We drive smaller cars and conserve energy. Most people would probably judge this impact to be negative. Yet, higher energy prices produced higher profit margins for the oil companies and their investors. People who make mass transit equipment or who are involved in developing alternative energy sources have benefited as well. Some analysts would even argue that higher prices now will help us avoid more serious problems when faced with the inevitable limits in non-renewable energy sources in the future.

It is also important to use information on local international activities to show students how they and people like them have an impact on people abroad. For example, newspapers should be searched for articles describing decisions or actions by local people, including inventions and research, which will have an impact abroad. These may not immediately appear to have an international dimension. However, because of the complex connections, some of them may ultimately improve or otherwise affect the lives of people abroad.

People: Local people who have international knowledge and experience or who were born in other countries provide an obvious resource for teaching students about the world. Bringing local people into the classroom in person can be particularly useful. Such people clearly demonstrate that the community, *and people like the students themselves,* are consciously involved in the world and have an impact on it. For example:

- In teaching about how people in the community make a living, or in career education at the secondary level, teachers can highlight the international aspects of jobs and careers whenever relevant. Someone can be invited to discuss the international dimensions of his or her career or international experiences while on the job.
- When dealing with other countries in geography, teachers can invite local people who have visited or lived in them to show slides and talk about the people and life there. For elementary classes, visitors can bring articles of clothing and other cultural artifacts. They can talk about the games children play, the songs they sing, what they study in school, and the role of children in the family.
- Teachers can invite people from a local business or a local college to talk about the community's linkages to other countries or areas abroad, emphasizing the impact of the community on the area, or the area's impact on the commmunity.
- In discussing current events or in courses in civics, American government, or Problems of Democracy, teachers can invite local people in political or service organizations to discuss their activities and perceptions of current global issues which affect the community.
- Teachers can invite someone associated with sister-cities or other special community programs to talk about what being a sister-city involves.
- In classes on American, state, or local history, teachers can have someone active in a local ethnic group demonstrate how the community's ethnic heritage affects life today.

Creating face-to-face encounters between students and people who were born abroad can do more to show students that people around the world are basically similar than any other learning experience short of living abroad. Such encounters can also expose students in a meaningful way to differing perspectives on issues and events. For example, teachers can:

- Invite a foreign student from a local university to talk about the effect of higher oil or energy prices on his or her country. A student from an OPEC country might share his or her perception of why OPEC leaders raised oil prices. A student from a non-oil-producing Third World country might talk about the problems that poorer countries face because of high oil prices.
- Invite a foreign student or visitor to talk about the problems of communicating across cultures. He or she could give examples of difficulties with English (e.g., idioms, subtle

differences between the formal and informal meanings of words) and explain subtleties of his or her native language which might give Americans trouble.
- Invite someone from the Middle East or Africa to talk about the Palestinian problem or about apartheid, focusing on the emotional side of these conflicts and issues as well as the facts.
- Invite a foreign student to talk about growing up in his or her home country, stressing what is similar as well as what is different.

Outside resource people will be most effective when their topics and visits are well-integrated into the ongoing curriculum, not just added on. Students should be prepared to ask questions, including controversial ones which reveal conflicting perspectives or biases of the speaker. At the same time, the interaction between resource people — particularly foreign visitors — and the class should extend beyond the formal classroom, if possible. Students might have lunch with the visitors in the school cafeteria. The visitor might be invited to stay for recess and play with the class on the playground. Opportunities to interact with foreign visitors in these settings are not always possible, but they can do much to provide an added opportunity for the visitor to tell about his or her country — and to learn from the students about life in America. They also provide opportunities for students to see foreign visitors as "people" who laugh, play, and eat just as they do.

While bringing local people into the classroom is an obvious strategy, locating people with relevant international experiences can pose problems for many teachers. Some communities do have speakers' bureaus or other programs which maintain files of available speakers and make initial contacts with them. A call to a local world affairs council or local hosting organization should suffice to find out if such a service is available. If not, a variety of other sources might be able to provide access to people with international involvements. These include the school system's own speakers' bureau or resource program, should it have one. Universities and colleges have world affairs experts and foreign students. Teachers might consider contacting the office of international programs, the foreign student office, the public relations department, or even the office of continuing education. Relevant business people can be found through the local chamber of commerce or by calling the public relations departments of major corporations in the community.

Before attempting to contact a resource person, however, teachers should know what type of person they want — e.g., foreign born or American born, business person, professor. They should also know what they want the resource person to do and how they want it done — e.g., topics, activities, and any resources or materials which the person should bring. A teacher may have to compromise on small details, but having a good idea of what is needed beforehand will help ensure that the resource person will meet the students' needs.

People in the community who do not have specialized international knowledge or experience can also serve as relevant sources of information for inquiry and critical thinking activities. For example, parents, grandparents, or other relatives can provide information on the class's international roots.

Using the questionnaire entitled "My Family's Migration History," teachers can:

- Have each student interview the oldest available member of his or her family and prepare a partial family tree to map that branch of the family's movements to the local community.
- Then, in groups, the class can map migration routes for different ethnic groups or peoples from different parts of the world as represented by the class.
- Finally, the information can serve as the basis for a discussion of the importance of mobility in a society. Reasons why current immigrant groups are coming to the United States and current shifts in population within the nation should be discussed.

MY FAMILY'S MIGRATION HISTORY

Interviewer_____ **Date**_____

Person Interviewed_____

Directions: Ask a member of your family to help you fill in the information about the history of your family's migration. The oldest available family member might be best able to help, but not necessarily. Note that, for each generation, you will need to fill in information for only *one* person. You will want to stay within the same family as you trace your family back, however (e.g., mother, mother's father, mother's father's father or mother). Get information on local birthplaces or hometowns when possible, but the state or even the country will do. *Go back until you get to someone who was born in another country*. Then stop!

Before you start the interview fill in as much of the information as you can:

Interview Questions

1. For a class project, I need to trace our family's history back to a family member who first came to the United States. Do you know the names and birthplaces of the following?

                                        Name   Birthplace or Hometown

    a. **You:** _____ _____

    b. **Your Parent** (either one): _____ _____

    c. **Grandparent:** _____ _____

    d. **Great-grandparent:** _____ _____

    e. **Great-great-grandparent:** _____ _____

    f. _____ : _____ _____

    g. _____ : _____ _____

    h. _____ : _____ _____

2. I would also like to know why those people moved, first to the United States and then around this country.

    a. When roughly did _____ (last person above) come to the United States and why?

    b. Why did the next generations move (if they did)?

"My Family's Migration History" traces only one side of the student's family, thereby avoiding embarrassment to students from one-parent households. Ethnic histories can also be embarrassing to students living with adoptive parents. An emphasis on the cultural influences of ethnic heritage — which touch all members of the household — can mitigate potential problems in this area.

Adults and even fellow students can also be used as resources for exploring local attitudes and policies respecting international activities. Since changes in the world have made us all participants in a global community, these attitudes and policies can be quite important. They affect the ways in which local people and organizations interact with the world. They determine how effectively local businesses compete and take advantage of international opportunities. They affect the responses of local people and groups to international problems which have an impact upon the community — e.g., higher oil prices, conflicts abroad, the arms race, the huge debts of Third World countries.

For example, investment by foreign corporations in the local community has increasingly been a source of considerable controversy in American communities. Teachers can:

- Direct students to conduct interviews using the questionnaire, "Attitudes Toward Foreign Investment," to probe local attitudes on this issue.
- In groups, the class can then discuss and prepare reports contrasting different sets of attitudes (e.g., attitudes toward investment in farmland versus investment in industry).
- The students should identify the kinds of stereotypes of foreigners which emerge from the interviews and discuss whether these stereotypes shape attitudes toward foreign investment more or less powerfully than strictly economic considerations.

ATTITUDES TOWARD FOREIGN INVESTMENT

To the Student: Before asking the following questions, explain that this interview is part of a lesson you are doing in social studies. The purpose of the lesson is to investigate different attitudes people have about foreign investment by businesses. Explain also that the interview should take about fifteen minutes and that it will be confidential. That is, no one but you will know who gave these particular answers.

1. Do you think our involvement with people around the world through business, tourism, and other activities is, generally speaking, good for the community?
   Yes_____ No_____ No Opinion_____
2. Why do you think so?
3. How do you feel about foreign businesses buying local farmland as an investment?
   Mostly good_____ Mostly bad_____ No Opinion_____
4. Why do you think so?
5. If a foreign firm were building a new factory and starting a new company locally would you see this as "mostly good" or "mostly bad" for the community?
   Mostly good_____ Mostly bad_____ No Opinion_____
6. Why?
7. Would it be mostly good or mostly bad if the foreign company were buying an existing local factory?
   Mostly good_____ Mostly bad_____ No Opinion_____
8. Why?
9. If a *local* company were trying to buy an existing factory in another country, do you think that would be mostly good or mostly bad for our community?
   Mostly good_____ Mostly bad_____ No Opinion_____
10. Why?
11. If an American company from another part of the country were buying a locally owned company or local farmland, would that be mostly good or mostly bad for the community?
    Mostly good_____ Mostly bad_____ No Opinion_____
12. Why?

At the end of the interview, thank the person for taking the time to share his or her ideas with you.

Attitude surveys such as these can be designed by the teacher or by the class around almost any current issue. In using them, however, teachers must exercise reasonable care. The surveys provide data on attitudes and policies. While they can help to identify basic issues, they probably will not provide information for resolving or even systematically analyzing those issues. However, looking at the survey data provides an opportunity for students to reflect on the views of people important to them — and to clarify their own views on issues which touch their lives and their communities. In the process, older students can learn something about the consistency of attitudes, and even the reasons why people hold the attitudes they do.

Survey instruments which probe attitudes on current issues must also be designed with care. Questions should be written unambiguously and pretested, if possible. The students should not return to the same sources too often. Even parents have limited tolerance for questionnaires. Students should be given opportunities to practice even simple interviews so that they can conduct them with confidence. Finally, it is typically best for students to survey only people with whom they are personally acquainted. Surveys of international leaders of the community, for example, can be extremely disappointing if the class contacts these individuals one week after another class has done so.

Organizations: Most urban communities have a vast array of organizations which participate in world affairs. Tapping community groups directly for instructional purposes can be useful, although more difficult than bringing a resource person into the classroom. Field trips to the zoo for elementary children or to museums and corporate headquarters for secondary students can be valuable, if somewhat costly. As with resource people, however, a context must be created which sensitizes students to the international dimensions of what they are seeing. Classroom work leading to and following the field trip should challenge students to question the implications of this organizational involvement in the world. Some organizations may not be appropriate for field trips. The League of Women Voters or the state's office of international trade, for example, may have extensive international involvements, but may afford little for a class of students to see. Thus, the time expended on the field trip might not be justified by the impact of the experience.

Other strategies for establishing contact with local organizations are available, however. As individual study projects, for example, students might visit or even work part time in an organization involved in some kind of international activity. As part of their observation experience, students would interview participants and report their experiences back to the class, with pictures and tape recordings, if possible. Students with an interest in an international issue can be encouraged to participate in related programs of a local organization, reporting to the class both on the issue and on the way in which the organization goes about addressing it.

Some community organizations can also be used for individual or small group field activities which are unobtrusive in nature. For example, students can:

- Visit a local department store and catalog products of various types — e.g., men's shirts, hand tools, toys — recording the countries of origin and prices of similar goods. They can calculate average prices for imports and average prices for goods produced in the United States. They should also look for any obvious features which distinguish imports from domestically produced goods — e.g., quality, advertised trademarks. On the basis of the data collected they can prepare reports which suggest how imports affect local consumers and producers in the United States.
- Visit a local grocery store and observe the types of goods which come from other countries and those which are domestically produced. During winter months, they might ask people in the produce section the origins of fresh fruits and vegetables. From these data, students can suggest the factors which might affect trade in food.

These types of activities provide opportunities to develop mathematical skills and also suggest some of the international dimensions of consumer and economics education.

While activities such as these may involve only a few students in the class directly, community organizations can also be investigated by the class as a whole through their publications and special reports. Sample literature on organizations, ranging from pamphlets describing the programs of voluntary groups to elaborate annual reports of business firms, can usually be obtained simply by telephoning the public relations department of the organization in question. Primary source materials such as these can be used to develop reading, critical thinking, and map skills, as well as to introduce students to the ways in which they and their community participate in the world. For example, students can:

- Compare and contrast the basic goals and concerns of different types of organizations — e.g., business firms, religious groups, civic organizations — using annual reports and other publications to infer those goals and concerns.
- Write or telephone to request the annual reports or brochures of several organizations concerned with a particular international issue — e.g., hunger, population, human rights. In small groups students can identify each group's response to the issue and decide which response they think would be most effective.
- Using annual reports of local business firms, younger students can prepare maps identifying where local companies are active in the world and briefly describe what local companies do internationally. The students can compare what the companies do abroad with what they do locally to see how international connections grow out of everyday activities.

Literature from organizations can be used with relatively young students in many cases. However, even with older students, the materials should be carefully screened by the instructor. Some, particularly from local business firms, will be too technical or will employ too much jargon to be useful. Some will simply be above the students' reading level. But most of these types of materials will be both readable and highly informative.

Conclusions

This chapter has described an agenda for teaching elementary and secondary students about the world. It has also described ways in which the community — that is, the people, organizations, and international activities that link the community to the rest of the world — might be used to achieve these objectives. These suggestions are hardly exhaustive. Yet, along with the social map of a typical community and its links to the world, they may provide not only some useful ideas, but a starting point for interested and creative educators to develop additional strategies.

Other sets of lessons and activity ideas which use the community as a resource in international education are also available. Two have been developed at the Mershon Center.[7] *World Regions: The Local Connection* includes lessons for teaching world geography and world cultures. The lessons are designed for middle school students, but most can be used with upper elementary classes, and some are appropriate for older students, as well. A second set of lessons, *Making Decisions: Our Global Connection,* provides an integrated unit on decision-making skills and concepts for grades 8–10, using local international activities as a substantive base. Other community-based programs have been developed in Stockton, California, and Evanston, Illinois. A model community-discovery program centered on individual research on community connections and community field trips has been developed and tested through American Field Service International's ANTHROS Project.[8]

Activity ideas using links between the states and the world have also been developed. Modeled after materials prepared by the Mid-America Program for Global Perspectives in Education at Indiana University, resource books are available for the following states: Arizona, Arkansas, Illinois, Indiana, Kentucky, Minnesota, New Mexico, Ohio, Oklahoma, and Vermont.[9]

Using the community as a resource for global education is not without challenges for teachers who would expose their students to the world in this way. However, the community provides a unique opportunity to demonstrate to students the relevance of the world to their lives and to their futures. The community and its global involvement provide a window on the world that can teach students not only about the global community, but also about their place in it.

---

[7]Both of the volumes described are published by the Columbus Council on World Affairs, 50 W. Broad Street, Suite 3220, Columbus, OH 43215.

[8]Information on these materials and programs, as well as others which use the community as a resource for global education, is available from the Citizenship Development Program, Mershon Center, 199 West Tenth Avenue, Columbus, OH 43201.

[9]Information on these materials is available from the Mershon Center, 199 West Tenth Avenue, Columbus, OH 43201, or from the Social Studies Development Center, Indiana University, 2805 East 10th Street, Bloomington, IN 47405.

CHAPTER III / MARK C. SCHUG

Approaches for Teaching Community Economics

A 1981 survey by Yankelovich, Skelly, and White concludes that the amount of economics education offered in the schools is increasing. According to the survey:
- Most teachers report that economics is introduced relatively early in the K–12 program. Two-thirds of junior high school economics teachers say that economics is available in the sixth and seventh grades.
- Approximately half of the teachers surveyed reported that economics is required in their schools.
- Students in 87 percent of the nation's junior and senior high schools can take economics.

There is also evidence that teachers are receiving more formal training in economics. Yankelovich et al. found that over 80 percent of teachers in grades 7–12 report having some training in economics. However, a study of teachers in Wisconsin (Schug, 1983) found that 44 percent of inservice elementary teachers and 60 percent of preservice elementary teachers have had no formal economics courses.

While the quantity of economics teaching apparently has increased, the quality of economics instruction is less certain. A persistent problem in teaching economics, either as a formal course or within other social studies courses, is finding concrete and meaningful ways to teach important economic concepts and principles. Economics is viewed by many students and teachers alike as an abstract and difficult area of study. The main purpose of this chapter is to suggest approaches for teaching economics which strive to make the abstract concrete and the dull interesting by focusing on the local community.

Economic Roles

It is obvious that the local community can provide numerous opportunities for studying our economic behavior. The economic activities of young people offer a good starting point. Youth are already important contributors to the local economy. Young people of all ages are consumers of goods and services. Children, for example, receive weekly allowances and make economic decisions about saving and purchasing. They accompany parents and friends to shopping malls, grocery stores, and discount outlets, where they observe buying and selling. In addition, the media regularly remind children of their importance as consumers and the influence that they have on the economic decisions of parents. Saturday morning television is filled with advertisements of toys, clothes, video games, bicycles, and sports equipment, all designed to appeal to young consumers. Children learn early, informally, of the importance of their role as consumers.

The consumer role of high school students is more prominent than that of elementary students largely because young people at this age have access to additional income through part-time employment. Greenberger and Steinberg (1981) report that since 1940, the proportion of 14- to 16-year-old males who work while attending school has increased five times. The increase for females has been even more dramatic. Current estimates are that over one-half of all high school juniors and seniors, and about 30 percent of all ninth and tenth grade students, are employed at one time during the school year. In addition, over 80 percent of all high school students will work before graduation. The same study also found that adolescents today work more hours than young people did 40 years ago. Over 50 percent of all 16-year-olds in the labor field work more than 14 hours per week. In addition to having enhanced their role as consumers, adolescents are making an increasing contribution to the local economy in their new role as workers.

There is also evidence that adolescents are increasingly active as entrepreneurs. For example, Steve Jobs and Steve Wozniak launched Apple Computers when they were still teenagers. Patton (1983) reports on other computer "whiz kids" with entrepreneurial instincts:

• At thirteen, Greg Hassett of Chelmsford, Massachusetts, wrote his first adventure game. The profits from Adventure World Company are now paying his way through college.

• David Gardner, sixteen, of Las Vegas, has been writing computer programs for several years and sells programs to a company called Simco.

• While a young teenager, Jonathan Rotenberg founded the Boston Computer Society, which today has 4,300 members and publishes a magazine with a circulation of 10,000. At fourteen, he had organized major computer shows and was chief programmer for Microfinance of Cambridge, Massachusetts. Currently, while in college, he does consulting jobs for $1,500 a day.

How do their economic experiences, especially part-time work, affect young people? Based on their survey of students in four California high schools, Greenberger and Steinberg (1981) concluded that students' work experiences promote some types of economic knowledge and a variety of other skills. Students with part-time jobs have opportunities to develop responsibility for assigned tasks and become more self-reliant. Young people who work in jobs which require extensive social contact, such as retail sales, learn to deal effectively with other people. Part-time work promotes the ability to persist in a task and obtain satisfaction from doing a good job. Finally, working enhances practical economic knowledge about business practices, finance, and consumer matters.

The work experiences of adolescents, however, have costs as well. Jobs open to young workers usually provide little contact with adults or opportunity for cooperating with others. More importantly, young workers do not usually feel that they make meaningful contributions to the organizations where they are employed. There is also evidence that working diminishes involvement in school and is associated with absenteeism. Working more than 15–20 hours per week may lead to a decline in school performance.

It is apparent that students' economic experiences are a factor in their economic education. In addition, young people make important contributions as workers and as consumers to the local economy. However, the finding that young workers do not feel that their contributions are meaningful to their employers is disconcerting. Ideally, the American economic system depends upon the active and informed involvement of the individual for its successful operation. Apparently, young people — at least in their roles as part-time workers — do not see the importance of their economic activity. Perhaps they do not recognize the importance of their future economic roles as producers, economic citizens, and members of labor unions. Young people often feel alienated from the political system. Evidence suggests that they feel alienated from the economic system, as well.

Strategies for overcoming the economic alienation of youth may not be easy to discover, much less to put into practice. Two approaches, however, are suggested (Schug, 1982a). The first involves developing a closer collaboration between the employers of young workers and educators to help shape the on-the-job experiences of young people and make them more meaningful. For example, educators and business people might participate in a series of local seminars designed to help major employers provide economic education for their young workers. The organizations of the firm, the decision-making process employed, and trends in the industry might be examples of topics which young workers and their employers might explore.

A second approach is to develop locally based curriculum materials which focus on the impact of individuals, such as young people, on the local economy. The Local Studies Project in Rochester, Minnesota, developed teaching activities and student materials to implement such an approach. An evaluation of the project found that student attitudes toward their roles in the local economy and their level of economic understanding improved (Schug and Beery, 1979). The following example illustrates how teachers can introduce this approach into the classroom.

YOUR MONEY AT WORK

1. Ask the students to record anonymously on a sheet of paper their estimate of the amount of money they spend and save each month.
2. Ask one student to use a calculator to add up the class's total spending and saving.
3. Record the figure on the board and ask the class to estimate the amount of money spent by all young people in their school and in their community each month.
4. Discuss with the class:
   a. What might happen to the local economy if all the people their age decided to stop spending their money?
   b. What are some examples of stores, restaurants, or financial institutions that might be affected?
   c. What decisions might each business have to make if the young population changed its spending or saving habits?

Teachers might assign the following projects to help students to learn more about the economic roles of young people.

YOU AS A CONSUMER AND A WORKER

- Keep a personal log of economic decisions you make each day for several days, including the weekends.
- Write a questionnaire asking about the economic activity of young people and administer it to your class or other classes in your school. What percentage of students work part time? At what jobs? How do they use their money? What types of businesses are most influenced by the spending of young people?
- Interview business people whose operation depends upon revenue from young people. Examples might be movie theatres, record shops, clothing shops, computer game arcades, and fast food restaurants. Ask about the creation of the business and the role of young people in it.
- Interview persons at the local employment office to explore problems of youth employment and government rules and regulations concerning employment of minors.
- If you work, interview your employer to find out why employers hire young people.
- Interview other students to discover why some young people choose to seek employment while others do not.

Community Economy

Another approach to community economics is to involve students in studying the economic life of their community. The current social studies curriculum provides little opportunity for students to analyze how the local community economy functions and how it may be changing. Yet, the local economy serves in many ways as a microcosm of the broader economy. It is possible to teach basic economic concepts such as scarcity, productive resources, interdependence, decision-making, and trade by referring concretely and directly to examples in the local community.

There are several types of approaches which can be used to help students study the local economy. These include the following:

Organizational Case Studies: Through formal curriculum development projects or through class activities, case studies can be developed which focus on economic enterprises in the local community. These case studies might focus on various types of firms, such as a small business, a multinational corporation, a manufacturer, a high technology company, or a farm cooperative. The content of the case studies can vary widely, but all should include information about the firm's past, changes in the firm over time, the number of its employees, and its relationships to the local, regional, national, and global economies. A variety of economic concepts might be emphasized, including scarcity, opportunity costs, productive resources, supply, demand, business cycle, technological change, and international trade. The Minneapolis Public Schools, for example, has developed a series of case studies of local firms and other economic organizations which are currently used by social studies teachers in the ninth and twelfth grades.

One case study in the series is entitled "Poppin' Fresh Pie Shops" and shows how a firm makes economic decisions about advertising, prices and wages, and site location. In one activity, students assume the role of Poppin' Fresh executives who must decide where to locate a new shop. Another case study, entitled "You Can Bank On It," focuses on a commercial bank in a low income area. Students play the roles of bank officers, depositers, and borrowers to learn aspects of how a commercial bank functions and the services it provides. "Graco — A Case Study on International Trade" presents the problems faced by a local firm involved in international trade. Students examine the development of the firm over time and make decisions about whether a product should be manufactured locally or in Japan.

Community Case Studies: Students might be encouraged to collect data about the local economy as a whole. Local census data and the chamber of commerce can often provide a great deal of useful information to help students or curriculum writers learn about local economic life. Some questions to help guide this research effort might include the following:

- Who are the major employers in the local community, in both the private and the public sectors?
- What are the strengths of the local economic base?
- What are the weaknesses or problems of the local economy?
- How does the local economy form an interdependent economic system locally, regionally, nationally, and internationally?
- How does the economic base influence the quality of life in the community?
- How are decisions on economic policy reached?
- What are the roles of firms, government, individuals, and groups in shaping local economic decisions?
- How are local economic institutions changing?

The following teaching activity might be used to introduce a study of the local economy.

1. Ask the students to guess the names of the largest employers in the local community. Write their speculations on the chalkboard.
2. Present the students with a list of the largest employers in the local community. A sample is provided below using the Milwaukee economy as an example.
3. Ask the students to classify the organizations into categories which describe their basic

function. The following categories might be helpful: manufacturing, retail, service, and wholesale.
4. Discuss with the class:
   a. Does our community economy seem to specialize in one form of economic activity?
   b. How might these economic enterprises depend upon one another?
   c. How might they depend upon economic activity in other communities, regions, or nations?

SELECTED LARGE EMPLOYERS IN MILWAUKEE: HANDOUT

1. Read through the list of selected employers below. Each of these local organizations employs more than 2,000 people. Not all employers of more than 2,000 people are included on the list.
2. Classify each organization according to its basic function by putting a letter next to the name of the employer. The following is one classification scheme you might wish to use.
   - M = Manufacturing
   - R = Retail
   - S = Service
   - W = Wholesale

AC Spark Plug Division GMC	(M)
Allen-Bradley Company	(M)
Allis-Chalmers Corporation	(M)
Briggs & Stratten Corporation	(M)
Good Samaritan Medical Centers	(S)
J.C. Penney Company, Inc.	(R)
Miller Brewing Company	(M)
Pabst Brewing Company	(M)
Rexnord, Inc.	(M)
Sears, Roebuck & Company	(R)
University of Wisconsin-Milwaukee	(S)
Wisconsin Electric Power Company	(S)

- Does it appear that the Milwaukee economy specializes in one form of economic activity? How?
- What are some ways that these economic organizations might depend on each other?
- How might these economic organizations depend on people in other cities, states, or parts of the world?

Community Economic History: Another way of studying the local economy is by focusing on the past. Barbara Reque (1983) reports on a curriculum development effort conducted by the DePaul Center for Economic Education. The purpose of this project was to develop a unit on Chicago's economic history. The focus of the unit was the fact that individuals affect and are affected by the economic changes in the local community. Information was collected about local industries, occupations, housing, transportation, communication, and the goods and services used by consumers. In addition, special attention was given to identifying individuals who were important in shaping Chicago's economic history. The result of all this work is a series of activity sheets to help students — independently or in small groups — study about Chicago's past.

Economic Field Experiences: Study of the local economy can be designed to give students firsthand experiences in local economic organizations. Arranging economic internships is one approach. For example, students might be given academic credit for taking a course entitled "Community Economics" which allowed them to spend time (one or two hours per day) as interns in economic organizations in the local community. An alternative might be to have students spend several hours a day over an intensive two-week period at the offices of an economic organization. The type of economic organizations selected for students would depend on the economic makeup of the local community. Examples include banks, manufacturers, multinational corporations, hospitals, retailers, professional sports, labor unions, government agencies, or insurance firms. Students also need an opportunity to meet regularly as a class to discuss and reflect on their experiences. While at the economic organization, the students should collect data to answer the following types of questions:

- How is the economic institution organized?
- What important functions does it perform?
- How does it make important economic decisions?
- What aspects of the economic organization make it unique?
- What major problems currently face the economic organization?
- How is it changing?
- How does the organization depend on other economic organizations?

Economic internships are intensive ways of involving students directly in the community economy. There are, of course, other less elaborate and more practical approaches as well. Field trips, for example, can be exciting experiences, enabling students to learn about basic economic ideas and processes. Advance planning is the key to any successful field trip. Attention needs to be paid to activities before, during, and after the field experience. Diane Reinke and Margit McGuire (1980) developed the following lesson for taking elementary students on a field trip to a factory. It is reproduced here to show how a field trip in economics can be carried out effectively.

A TRIP TO A FACTORY

Grade level: Elementary
Skill: Research — locating information
Economic Concept: Productive resources — factors of production
Data Source: The environment — a field trip
Introduction: Students practice observing and listening by taking part in a trip to a manufacturing plant. To benefit from the activity, students should have had prior experience in using these skills.
This lesson can be integrated into elementary social studies units on manufacturing as it takes place in a variety of geographical settings.
Objective: Students will listen and observe in order to gain information about productive resources by:
1. Participating in a field trip to a factory;
2. Answering assigned questions;
3. Drawing and labeling pictures of three of the productive resources seen on the field trip.

Materials: Handout

Procedures:
1. Plan the trip.
   a. Obtain permission from the school principal or other responsible school official.
   b. Contact the factory you wish to visit. Select a plant in which students can easily see and recognize the productive resources used in the manufacturing process. Be sure to provide the business with the following written information:
      (1) Date and time of arrival.
      (2) Purpose of the visit.
      (3) Description of your class — grade level, number of students, number of adults, etc.
      (4) Specific information that students are to learn — explain to contact person that students are to practice listening and observing by looking for and describing the productive resources used in the business.
      (5) Length of time of the visit.
   c. Become acquainted with the facility by visiting it prior to the field trip.
   d. If the guide will be someone from the business, give the person a copy of the handout.
   e. Arrange for transportation.
   f. Prepare and send permission slips home with students.
   g. Arrange for adults to accompany students on the trip. Tell the adults what their duties will be on the trip. (Plan a ratio of not more than eight children to one adult.)
   h. Plan to return to school in enough time to discuss what was learned on the trip.
   i. Call the business the morning of the field trip to remind them of your impending visit.
2. Prepare students for the field trip.
   a. Explain to students that they will be taking a trip to visit a business. Tell them what the business is called and what product it manufactures.
   b. Explain the purposes of the trip:
      (1) To observe how people work together in producing a product;
      (2) To observe the productive resources used in the business;
      (3) To listen to the guide describe how productive resources are used in the business.
   c. Define terms the students will hear used on the field trip:
      (1) Productive resources
      (2) Natural resources
      (3) Human resources
      (4) Capital goods resources
   d. Discuss appropriate behavior for the field trip. Have students practice appropriate behavior — e.g., take the class for a walk around the school.
3. The trip.
   a. Assign each adult to a specific group of students
   b. Assign each group specific questions from the handout to report on when the class returns from the trip. Read the questions aloud to be sure everyone in the group understands them. Students and adults should take copies of the questions with them on the trip to refer to as needed.
   c. Allow time just before the trip to:
      (1) Review the purposes of the trip and the questions each group is to answer.
      (2) Review appropriate behavior.
   d. During the visit, help students to practice their observing and listening skills by asking appropriate questions. If the presentation is too advanced, restate it in terms your students can understand. (Remember that guides often have had little experience in talking to young children.)
4. Follow-up activities.
   a. Ask each of the groups to meet and discuss its questions. Encourage the adults to stay and assist their groups in this activity. Select a reporter for each of the groups.

b. Have groups answer their assigned questions. Have reporters give presentations to the entire class.
c. Ask additional questions that will reinforce the skills being practiced.
d. To provide closure, ask students to draw pictures of three productive resources seen at the factory. Ask them to label the productive resources (natural resources, human resources, capital goods resources) in their pictures.
e. Have students write thank-you notes to the manufacturer. You may want to help students start their notes with the following sentence: "On the trip to (name of business) I learned . . ." You may also want to send some of the pictures drawn by the students.

A TRIP TO THE FACTORY: HANDOUT

GROUP 1
1. What does this business do?
2. What skills did you use to help you decide what this business does?

GROUP 2
1. Name three capital goods that this factory uses.
2. How did you learn about these three goods on the trip?

GROUP 3
1. Name three natural resources that this factory uses.
2. What skills did you use to help you identify the natural resources?

GROUP 4
1. What skills do you think the employees need in order to do their jobs?
2. What skills did you use to help you answer question 1?

GROUP 5
1. How do you think the employees learned to do their jobs?
2. What jobs would take the longest to learn?

GROUP 6
1. Do you think the employees like their jobs?
2. What did you see or hear that would tell you whether or not the employees liked their jobs?

David E. O'Connor (1983) presents another idea for economic field experiences. In this approach, high school students use Old Sturbridge Village — a living museum in southern Massachusetts — as a rich resource for learning about economic ideas in a historical context. The economic content of the program revolves around three basic questions:
- What to produce and how much to produce?
- How to produce?
- For whom to produce?

After warm-up activities to get students thinking about work and making a living today, students are divided into four groups to learn how people made a living in the past. Students visit the businesses at the museum and then participate in a variety of tasks, including making prints from wall stencils and producing wooden mallets. Museums, as illustrated by this example, can also be used in innovative ways to teach basic economic concepts.

Funding for Community Economics

Many of the activities described in this chapter were developed as curriculum projects which received special funding from a variety of private and public sources. It is not surprising that local businesses, foundations, and government agencies take an interest in involving young people in the economic life of the community. Some organizations view community economics programs as a way of promoting pro-business attitudes among young people, in addition to improving their economic understanding. A common outcome of community-based programs is that teachers, students, and business people have fewer stereotypes of one another. Teachers and students involved in community economics programs begin to understand the risks, complexities, and difficult decisions that business people face. Business people, on the other hand, gain new respect for the problems which teachers face in their day-to-day work with young people.

Social studies educators, concerned about having a balanced K–12 economics program, are justifiably worried about funded projects which may be little more than efforts to promote one economic point of view instead of a balanced presentation of economic issues and problems. Nonetheless, social studies leaders are often interested in working with local or state funding sources when there is agreement on the goals and objectives of the project. How can social studies educators be sure a funded community economics project is educationally sound?

The following six criteria (adapted from Schug, 1982b) may help curriculum writers in developing community economics programs which will attract funding from private sources.

1. Does the curriculum project have citizenship education as a primary goal? One dimension of citizenship education is the need to be informed about economic issues and trained in using decision-making skills. Because economic interpretations vary widely, it is also important that students learn and practice critical thinking skills such as distinguishing fact from opinion, distinguishing inference from fact, and identifying opinions, biases, and value judgments.

2. Does the project emphasize basic economic concepts and generalizations? Unfortunately, many curriculum efforts lack a clear conceptual focus. The best efforts are those that emphasize broad concepts that can be learned and reinforced throughout the K–12 program and that are not subject to short-term changes.

3. Does the project recognize more than one economic interpretation? Some special interest groups defend the free enterprise system as being faultless, while others accuse the economic system of exploitation and domination by "big business." While materials which expose a particular point of view are worthwhile for teaching critical thinking skills, the objective of a commu-

nity economics program should be to provide a balanced approach that fairly represents differing viewpoints.

4. Does the project enhance the quality of instruction? The methods used to teach a subject often determine whether any learning will occur. The community economics project should encourage variety in instructional methods, including simulations, class discussions, field trips, films, transparencies, and role-play activities. In addition, the project should emphasize important contemporary issues, such as recession, economic growth, and unemployment.

5. Does the project have an adequate evaluation plan? Clearly, curriculum materials which involve field-testing in several classrooms are more effective than those that are not. In addition, it is useful to provide for more elaborate evaluation, including adequate designs for measuring understanding before and after instruction, and control groups.

6. Does the community economics project serve to enhance local curriculum goals? Obviously, curriculum development efforts which run counter to the goals or objectives of the local social studies K–12 curriculum should not be undertaken.

Summary

This chapter has suggested that economic instruction can be improved by focusing on the local community. Young people's economic experiences as workers and consumers is a useful foundation upon which to build an economics program that can be extended by studying the local economy and developing economic field experiences. Such curriculum efforts are often supported by private funding sources and thus require extra care to ensure that the materials produced are balanced. To be worthwhile, a project should emphasize citizenship education, instruction of high quality, an adequate plan of evaluation, and local curriculum goals.

Teachers interested in initiating a community economics program should consider the following suggestions:

• Meet with other social studies teachers to discuss their interest in using a community-based approach for teaching economics.

• Conduct an assessment of social studies students' understanding of economic ideas. The *Basic Economics Test* (grades 4–6) and the *Test of Economic Literacy* are useful instruments. They are published by the Joint Council on Economic Education and can be obtained at little cost. Data from the assessment are useful for determining the level, scope, and need for a community economics project.

• Establish an advisory committee with representatives from business, labor, and agriculture, as well as teachers and administrators. Purposes of the advisory group include helping to formulate goals for a community economics

project, identifying potential sources of funding, and identifying local instructional resources.
- Contact your state council or center for economic education affiliated with the Joint Council on Economic Education to discuss ideas and identify available resources.
- Contact other key individuals and organizations in the community which may have an interest in community economics program. The chamber of commerce, local labor board, and major employers might be good initial contacts to assist in planning the program.

Bibliography

Greenberger, E., and Steinberg, L. D. "Part-Time Employment of In-School Youth: A Preliminary Assessment of Costs and Benefits." Program on Social Ecology, University of California at Irvine, June, 1981.

National Survey of Economics Education. Yankelovich, Skelly, and White, Inc., 1981. (Copies available from Playback Associates, 708 Third Avenue, New York, NY, 10017.)

O'Connor, D. E. "Learning About the American Economy Through Living Museums," *Social Education,* January 1983, 40–43.

Patton, P. "The Computer Business is Child's Play." *Republic Scene,* February 1983, 41–42, 74–75.

Reinke, Diane, and McGuire, Margit. *The Book Company.* Washington State Council on Economic Education, Office of the Superintendent of Public Instruction, 1980.

Reque, B. "Making Choices: Studying Your Community's Economic History," *Social Education,* January 1983, 32–35.

Schug, M. C. *Economic Education Across the Curriculum.* Fastback Series. Bloomington, IN: Phi Delta Kappa Foundation, 1982.

———. "Elementary Teacher's Views on Economic Issues," *Theory and Research in Social Education,* Spring, 1983.

———. "Teaching High School Economics Based on Student Economic Experiences," *Social Studies,* January/February, 1982, 8–11.

Schug, M. C., and Beery, R. W. "Developing a Responsive and Responsible Community Based Economics Curriculum." *Phi Delta Kappan,* November 1979, 214–215.

Weidenaur, D. H. (Chair). *Using Economics in Social Studies Methods Courses.* New York: Joint Council on Economic Education, 1982.

CHAPTER IV / R. BEERY

State History and Community Study

They trudged along on a crisp October morning, each with a copy of a very old sketch map. Now they headed up the bank of the river toward Court House Hill trying to figure out where the trading post must have been; and the chapel, the mill, and the stockage. The river's course had apparently shifted over the last century. But they thought they had located the old landing, now the resting place for old tires, a couple of corroded oil drums, and a rusty bed spring.

"My great-great-grandma, she's *really* old — ninety-six. Well, when I got her going did she have a story to tell! She had lived in a kind of cave house when her family first came from Norway. Wow! She talked about the bugs, mice, snakes, and grasshoppers that got into everything. And work! She helped out in the fields when she was ten years old. When she was even younger she had to babysit, work in the garden, gather wild berries, hang out wet clothes to dry — even in the winter. I mean, she really worked *all* the time! Anyway, I never really talked to her before — really talked to her — about *her* life."

The big kid in the torn jersey had complained all the way out on the bus. He didn't want to go to a cemetery in the middle of nowhere, not if it meant being late for practice. It seemed like another dumb idea. He went along half-heartedly with the others who were gathering information from the headstones. Then he found one with a strange sounding name — Geitzenhauer. He used to know a kid with that name. Interesting. The other smaller stones right next to the one that caught his eye were worn, couldn't be read clearly. Soon he was working on one of them with butcher paper and an oversized crayon — rubbing out a message that was becoming clearer, but still not very understandable. What language was it? He intended to find out.

Young people actively exploring a landscape, handling artifacts, and discovering people from an unknown past are experiencing history. This can happen at any grade level. The primary school student can develop a personal sense of the past by trying on old clothing, using hand tools such as apple peelers and cornhuskers, and listening to delightful tales of childhoods past. These activities can be part of a class visit to a local historical society.

During the intermediate years, when state history is a central curricular concern, emphasis on change in recent decades provides many opportunities for firsthand encounters with the past. Photographs, maps, school records, and census data for 1960, 1970, and 1980 can be valuable starting points for studying history close to students in time and place. The sense of having been a part of history and of an ever-changing present can capture the young imagination and breathe life into the study of the past. Moving beyond this very personal perspective, intermediate students can explore material in depth on the development of key communities in the state.

Secondary school surveys in U.S. history can be enriched and enlivened by concrete references to life in the local area as examples of broader national events and trends. There are key historical times when the local community captures the essence of broader state and national history. For example, the founding of every community is an event of historical significance that can only be understood in terms of national trends.

State Study, by the Book

School children study their own state at least once in every social studies program, usually during the middle school years. The quality of this effort depends upon the teacher. If textbooks receive the greatest emphasis in state study, there is room for serious concern. While texts frequently hint at an interdisciplinary approach, state study most often proceeds chronologically. First, students learn about geography — the "stage" upon which the state's history was subsequently enacted. The state's geography tends to be viewed as a marvelous set of resources waiting to be used by deserving colonists or pioneers. The cultures of native peoples are usually presented as colorful ways of life that prevailed long ago; they are idealized and stereotyped. When students learn about the establishment of the state's government, they may be taught something about the structure and functions of that government today. As they encounter various ethnic groups in the chronology, they usually learn about an array of highly visible cultural characteristics, including foods and festivals. These ethnic survivals are frequently presented as quaint diversions, vestiges that may flavor daily life in incidental and harmless ways. Economic development is usually treated historically and is tied to particular entrepreneurs and colorful groups such as lumberjacks, cowboys, homesteaders, and miners.

This method of teaching state history can be a pageant full of action and color, but it frequently romanticizes and distorts the relative significance of the state. This type of state history aims to be a series of adventure stories suitable to the age level of the students. This approach does not engage students in actively relating to their own part of the state. In general, students are not directed to use these colorful adventures to build understandings of change, continuity, and conflict, or to explore and respond to the moral clashes that underline many of these heroic tales. There is often a failure to bring the past to bear in consideration of present problems. National context and global setting tend to be minimized or ignored.

The most serious problem with these materials, however, may be their message of historical inevitability — the subtle implication that things happened as they were supposed to happen — that the state's progress through time was as it should have been, and is as it should be. Problems are too commonly seen as minor difficulties which have tested the strength and intelligence of the state's virtuous people and courageous leaders.

State and Communities

This chapter suggests that we approach study of the state with two kinds of community study. First, segments from the histories of particular communities in various parts of the state provide useful case studies for detailed consideration of significant developments. Second, the local community offers a useful context for actively developing skills, perspectives, concepts, and sensitivities involving history as a sequence of events created by people.

This approach emerged in the process of searching for fresh approaches to state history in Minnesota. This endeavor, Minnesota Community Studies, a Title IV C project, uses five communities as case studies and structures exploration of the student's own community in the present, the past, and the future.

The assumption that state history should be a chronological survey is subject to question. If students examine the past in key communities in some depth, they will develop a fuller understanding of the meaning of change. The chronology of the state does not capture the overwhelmingly local quality of life down through the nineteenth century. In a sense, history is always local. To understand settlement of any of our states is to understand processes of community formation. The state is but a broader framework of institutions that facilitates the processes that take place within the community.

It should be clear at the outset that the intent of this approach is to use the past selectively and in an interdisciplinary manner to develop key skills and understandings. Skills, concepts, processes, and understandings, as well as intuitions, emotions, and personally felt attachments, are all recognized as valuable outcomes of local and state studies which draw upon community, family, and self.

Community Case Studies

Minnesota Community Studies case materials are briefly described here in order to suggest ways that the notion of community can be used to teach selective history while developing concepts and skills within an interdisciplinary focus. A variety of materials and strategies are employed in these case studies. Included are narrative readings, filmstrips, presentations of value dilemmas, suggestions for role-playing, census data, audiotapes of interviews, photographs, and primary source materials, such as diaries and letters. Descriptions of the five community case studies follow:

Community Growth is a four-week exploration of Rochester, Minnesota, as a frontier center in the westward migration, regional retail center today, home of the internationally significant Mayo medical complex and site of a major IBM facility. Concepts emphasized are migration, economic interdependence, and community change.

Living in the City, a three-week unit, emphasizes the lively and dynamic Chicano/Mexican-American community in St. Paul, by exploring concepts of community as metropolitan area and neighborhood, cultural change as exemplified in life history materials, and voluntary participation in political processes.

Two Communities is a two-week unit which compares and contrasts the different ways in which two societies — Northern European immigrants and the Santee Dacotah people — saw and used the rich natural environment of the Minnesota River Valley. The relationship between perceptions and behavior is examined, as well as the role of cultural perceptions in generating conflict. Cultural change is considered within two contemporary communities — predominantly German-American New Ulm and the Lower Sioux Community — while the significance of ethnic identity and changing patterns of ethnicity are considered.

Change on the Range, a two-week unit, compares and contrasts values, technologies, and behaviors of distinct groups who have made their home in northeastern Minnesota. Economic interdependence — national and international — is used to explain the "boom and bust" quality of the Mesabi Iron Range's history. Conflicting perspectives on land use are examined in a role-play activity dealing with future development of known copper and nickel reserves. The rich ethnic mix that has dominated range life since the late nineteenth century is highlighted.

Rural Minnesota is a two-week unit focusing on the town and agricultural base of Benson to emphasize interdependence and changing agricultural patterns. The dominant focus of this unit is on life today.

The Minnesota Community Studies approach to the state and to history is not comprehensive. Minnesota is not "covered" chronologically or geographically. Case materials do not result in a clear understanding of the state as an entity with boundaries, places, topographical features, and resources. Also, the state is not presented as a political/legal/governmental jurisdiction.

Identifying State Communities

To develop case studies such as these, communities and people involved in them can be selected to reflect key characteristics, trends, and episodes in a state's past. This content will not necessarily focus on the episodes or persons that figure in local mythologies or the colorful and bizarre legends which lure tourists to the state.

Appropriate communities for focused study about your state should reflect particular historical experiences. Community studies for Florida, Vermont, Virginia, Oregon, and the others should be very different from the studies outlined here in Minnesota. Whether one needs to build an entire course of study "from scratch" or merely wishes to supplement a text with community cases, the first concern is to find appropriate content and identify materials potentially valuable for student use.

The need to select significant sample communities and the need to find or create student materials of quality usually work together in determining the cases that are developed. Communities selected should exemplify key kinds of settlements within the state's past. For example, an early Puritan town would need to be included in Massachusetts. The particular community selected would depend upon the print and visual materials which were available and adaptable for student use. In addition, it is appropriate to seek communities from various parts of the state to help highlight different periods in the state's past and to reflect diversity and ongoing cultural change.

Instructional Goals

There is a need to build case materials around skills and concepts to be learned. These can give focus and direction to student activities and materials. Without this kind of deliberate structure, case studies can become colorful entertainment with little educational value. Goals can be drawn from those established by the local school district or the state. The Minnesota Community Studies project, for example, focused on the development of "inquiry and valuing processes" from the goals of the Minnesota Assessment of Education Progress, which had been derived from those established by the National Assessment of Educational Progress. It was decided that content, materials, and activities would be selected and developed to promote these skill and process goals.

The Minnesota Community Studies project was organized around six concepts — those used by both the Minnesota and the National Assessment of Educational Progress (1975-76 Assessment). These emphasize social organization, social environments, physical environments, decision-making, conflict and values.

Ethnicity was not explicitly identified as a separate conceptual area, but it became a dominant theme in the community case materials. Dimensions of ethnicity were explained or clarified as material with ethnic content was developed for presenting St. Paul's Mexican-American community, the Santee Dacotah today and in the past, the Ojibwe in various cultural contact situations, the dynamic Mesabi mining communities, and the German-Americans at New Ulm.

Where resources are available for major curriculum development, teachers are urged to develop detailed case materials as an alternate course of state study. The individual teacher might more readily supplement a survey text with brief community case studies, gradually including more and more cases and expanding each case as new materials allow. While the Minnesota Community Studies project focused on extended community cases, it might be more appropriate in other instances to develop briefer cases with a sharper focus on concepts or skills. For example, a teacher might start with four or five photographs from a particular time and place, adding readings, a map, and other visuals, as they become available.

Making Personal Connections

It is important to engage students in thoughtful explorations of their own lives as members of a family, students at a specific school, members of particular peer groups, and participants in specific neighborhoods. These explorations involve focusing on development of particular aspects of each individual's identity. This task requires explicit attention to the subtle, unconscious, "natural" learning of behaviors that are the basic elements of one's communities. Here, the student's attention shifts from studying case materials about other communities to making his or her own exploration of community.

This kind of inquiry into the past begins with the individual's own history and moves back in time, adding a historical dimension to the young person's awareness of self. It should be clear that this is *not* intended simply to be an opportunity to apply broad concepts, nor is it intended primarily as a setting for carefully guided discovery of generalizations explaining human behavior. On the other hand, concepts and generalizations, as well as information about the past and the place, are actively *used* by the individual in building a historical conception of self. The conscious development of explanations of one's connections with others over time is worthwhile in and of itself. It is an important intellectual and emotional experience that is seldom emphasized inside or outside of the public schools.

The following teaching activities are only a beginning for enhancing the student's sense of personal connection with history. The achievements of this school-based effort are inherently individual and humane. These experiences should be viewed as stimulating vital personal growth, with an understanding of history, state history, social science, and social studies ranking second in degree of importance. Nevertheless, this stimulus can be the basis for genuine involvement with history and other dimensions of social education throughout life.

Personal history activities can help students to experience the nature of history. Scientists assume that they need to perform a variety of experiments in order to develop knowledge, especially knowledge of science as a process. The activities that follow suggest different levels at which the processes of historical work can be experienced.

Student motivation should not be overlooked. Much as been made of the decline of history in the schools, colleges, and universities. At the same time that enrollments in history classes have declined, historical fiction, family history and genealogy, and local history have flourished. The activities presented here are ways to capture and extend the natural interest in what is personal and near at hand.

Personal history activities can help to stimulate creativity. All too often, there is little individuality in history and social studies. Concepts, skills, and data must be learned, but the kind of personal involvement that characterizes such areas as writing, art and woodworking is often lacking.

The activities that follow are not new. They are adapted from a rich tradition of lively history projects that have been developed to incorporate active learning into the study of history. Also, the new interest in social history has focused attention on these kinds of activities in recent years. Perhaps what is new here is the insistence that this is the kind of study that should be the heart of state history and that, in the proper context, it has much more to offer than simply stimulating interest.

The activity that follows is aimed at initiating exploration of the individual student's own experiences and using those experiences as useful sources of historical information.[1]

YOU ARE HISTORY!

You have stories about your life in the past. You have experienced change. You can answer questions about your changing past. You are a source of information. YOU ARE HISTORY.
Let's take some time to explore ourselves as history:

1. *Some Private History.*
   a. Take out a piece of paper and a pencil or pen.
   b. Make sure it is completely quiet so you can think.
   c. Make sure you have some private space to work in.
   d. *What you write is personal and will not be turned in and does not have to be shared in discussion.*
   e. All set?
   f. **Do This:** Write ten (10) statements that answer the question WHO AM I?[*] (You know: I am a sister . . . I am a paper carrier . . .) Often the most important things about you do not come out first. They come only after serious thought. So try very hard to think of the statements about who you are.

2. *A Discussion.* Okay. As usual, you're going to *discuss* ideas that come from your WHO AM I? statements. Yes, we said you wouldn't have to show or tell anybody what you included in your ten statements. And we meant it! So, if a question seems personal, you can decide not to respond. Just listen and see what you can learn from the others!

   a. How many wrote something about being part of the neighborhood or community? Statements like:
      I am a West Sider.   I am a person who lives in Texas.
   b. How many wrote down something to do with being part of a family?
      I am a Johnson.   I am a sister.

---

[*]History is questions and this is an important question — maybe the most important history question because it's about your own history.

[1]This exercise is an adaptation of material in "Looking at Our Community" © Minnesota Community Studies Project (Rochester, MN: 1978). Used with permission.

c. How many wrote down something to do with being part of an ethnic group — a group based on the background of you or your ancestors?
I am Norwegian.   I am Hmong from Laos.
I am Jewish.   I am Cherokee.
d. Decide which of your ten statements is most important in telling who you really are. If you feel comfortable about it, share your response with the class. Whether you share or not, think about this most important WHO AM I? statement. Does your most important statement have to do with family? Is it related to the past, your life in the past?

YOU ... FAMILY ... HISTORY

Each of you has had a different past. It's that past, your own personal history, that makes you a very special, unique person. And yet we've all had some of the same kinds of experiences. Some of the most important experiences in our lives are those that have to do with *family*.

Each of us is part of a family. You live with and depend on at least one other person. There are two ways you become part of a family: you are born into the family *or* you join by adoption, marriage, or being asked to live with the family.

You also consider grandparents, aunts, uncles, and cousins part of your family, even though you probably don't live with them.

Now you are going to find out some interesting information about your family so that you can think some more about WHO YOU ARE and about CHANGE OVER TIME. You will have a chance to share what you find out about yourself in class discussion. Because all of this information is personal, you will not have to share anything you don't want to. The important thing is private, anyway. We want you to learn more about a very important person — YOU!

To get started, fill in the ME blanks (Name, Year Born, Place of Birth). You will probably need some help from a member of your family as you fill out a chart like the one on the next page. (By the way, we know the tree is a bit strange. Don't make a fuss about it. Draw a better one!)

FAMILY BACKGROUND

You can answer some of these questions by thinking about your daily life. You can answer others with the chart. Discuss others with your family. Write the answers in sentences.
1. What places (cities, provinces, countries, continents) did your ancestors come from?
2. Where does your name come from?
3. Does your family eat any special foods associated with the places your ancestors came from?
4. Does your family belong to a special religion practiced in the place your ancestors came from?
5. Does your family celebrate any special holidays important in the places your ancestors came from? If so, name them.
6. Does your family have any books, clothing, furniture, works of art, or other things that belonged to your ancestors? If so, list them.
7. Think about your answers. Decide whether the old ways of doing things make a difference in your family life today. Explain.

YOUR FAMILY ROOTS

1. Who was the first member of your family who lived in this community?
2. Why did that person come here?
3. Explain some of the ways the community has changed since then.

A YOU PROJECT

Write a paragraph that tells some of the special ways that your family history has affected your life. Remember: history deals with stories about the past and changes in the ways people live. So, what are some important happenings in your family's past that have changed the ways members of your family (including you) have lived?

STATE HISTORY AND COMMUNITY STUDY 49

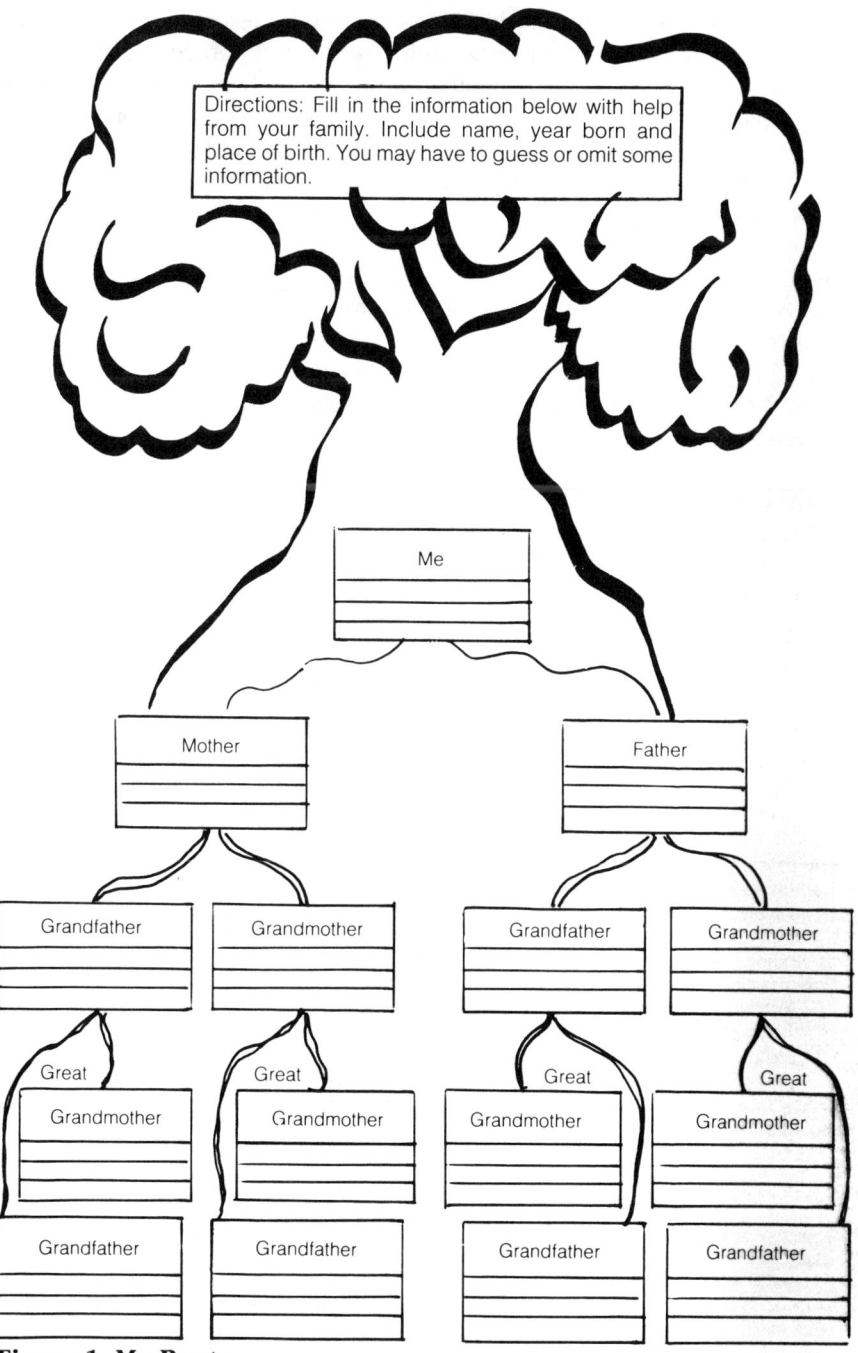

Directions: Fill in the information below with help from your family. Include name, year born and place of birth. You may have to guess or omit some information.

Me

Mother

Father

Grandfather

Grandmother

Grandfather

Grandmother

Great Grandmother

Great Grandmother

Great Grandmother

Great Grandmother

Grandfather

Grandfather

Grandfather

Grandfather

Figure 1. My Roots

Family trees are used a great deal in studying family history. One sophomore complained that she had made a family tree in sixth-grade social studies, seventh-grade geography, and eighth-grade American history, and she did not think that she needed the same assignment again! Purposes of these assignments need to be explicit. Information collected should be clearly directed toward developing particular ideas, as well as gathering facts about the individual and his or her past.

A variety of other activities can emphasize family as a source of interesting historical information. Students can compile scrapbooks from family records, learn about crafts or skills in which older family members are proficient, and research the history of artifacts treasured by their families. Students might record family stories and favorite songs, examine old photographs for evidence of outmoded customs, and write biographies of especially interesting ancestors.

Interviewing for Information

Students can conduct interviews with family members and other people in the community as an effective way of gathering historical information. Conducting an interview is a complex activity, involving many kinds of knowledge and skills. Students will need to be carefully prepared to conduct successful interviews. The following two handouts were developed to introduce interviewing techniques to high school students. The first one prepares students to interview family members. It helps students to select a topic to focus upon in the interview, and stresses the need for sensitivity and tact in questioning about certain areas of family life.

FAMILY INTERVIEW TOPICS AND QUESTIONS[2]

The most interesting interviews focus on things the person you are talking to has actually experienced. Usually a good interview is limited to one topic. This allows the person to spend time on lively details. For example, rather than trying to cover all aspects of a grandparent's life, you might focus on your grandfather's experiences as a tank driver in World War II or your grandmother's experiences as an 18-year-old country school teacher in rural North Dakota.

The questions you ask during an interview will determine the quality of your family history.

The following topics may give you some ideas which you would like to explore. Narrow the topic and questions whenever possible. For example, you may wish to focus on Christmas in your family rather than deal with holiday traditions generally.

The particular topic and questions you choose to explore should depend upon the person you talk to and your own interests. It is important that you spend time developing good questions before you do your interview.

---

[2]These activities are adapted from questions prepared by the Family Folklore Program, Smithsonian Institution, Division of Performing Arts, January 1976, and "Writing the Social History of One's Family: Guidelines for Faculty Members and Students," reprinted in *Social Education*, October 1977, p. 480.

FAMILY QUESTIONS

Names
1. What do you know about your family surname? Its origin? Its meaning? Did it undergo change coming from the "Old Country" to the United States? Are there stories about the change?
2. Are there any traditional first names, middle names, or nicknames in your family? Is there a naming tradition, such as always giving the first son the name of his paternal grandfather?

Traditions
1. What are some special family traditions associated with holidays? Where and how did these traditions get started?
2. How have special traditions changed from one generation to another? What are the reasons for these changes?

Love and Marriage
1. How did your parents or grandparents come to meet and marry?
2. Are there any romantic tales about unusual courtships, elopements, or runaway lovers?
* 3. Are there any stories about individuals who ran away from their wives or husbands and children? What about divorces?

Family Life
1. Who lived with the family?
2. How were decisions made in the family?
3. How were babies treated in the family?
4. At what age was a young person expected to take on adult responsibilities?
5. What were attitudes towards elderly family members?
6. Were family ties strong or weak? Were reunions held? Did relatives visit one another frequently? How were weddings and funerals observed?

Education and Careers
1. What kind of education did family members have?
2. At what age did they go to work on their own?
3. Why did they take up the jobs that they did?
4. What was the family attitude toward work by women?

Ties to "Big History"
1. How did historical events affect the family — the Great Depression, the Civil War, or the war in Vietnam?
2. Why did your ancestors come to America? What experiences or events back "home" and in America led to the decision to come here?
3. Why and how did your family come to this state?

Unusual Stuff
1. Are there any special family tales or jokes that have been passed down over the generations?
2. Are there any special characters in your family? What can you find out about them?
* 3. Are there certain things about which no one in your family will talk?
* 4. Are there any family conflicts or feuds that have lingered on for many years? Can you find out the "hows" and "whys" of these?
* 5. Are there any "skeletons" in your "family closet"? What can you find out about them?

---

*Be careful if you explore these topics. Be sensitive to people's feelings when you ask questions and don't report anything that might embarrass family members.

The second handout on interviewing included here prepares students to interview people in the local community. It gives them specific advice on choosing a topic and formulating questions. It also outlines a protocol for students to follow in arranging and conducting an interview. Students may need to spend some time practicing interviewing. Having students interview one another in class is often a good way to get them started.

INTERVIEWING[3]

A. **Starting Up**
Select a topic of special interest to you. The most interesting interviews happen when people are telling about their own experiences. People usually like to talk about their high school years, their families, their jobs, and other personal experiences.

1. Keep questions short and clear.
2. Ask questions that focus on *Who?*, *What?*, *When?*, *Where?*, *Why?*, and *How?*
3. Prepare open-ended questions rather than questions that can be answered with one word. For example, "What did you like most about school?" will lead to more information than "Did you like school?"

Arrange for an interview by calling the person on the phone to make an appointment. Be sure to identify who you are, why you want the interview, and the time and place when you would like to do it. Give the person your name, your teacher's name, and a phone number where you can be reached (in case he or she has to cancel the interview or will be late).

If you plan to use a tape recorder, be sure the person being interviewed does not object to being taped. Then, be sure to check your equipment and make sure it's in working order before going to the interview.

B. **Doing It**
It's best to be alone with the person you are interviewing. Begin with a few minutes of "small talk" to relax the person you are interviewing.

Explain what you are going to do. If you do use a recorder, show the person how it works. Explain that you will be taking notes.

Take brief notes.

Ask one question at a time.

Keep your questions brief.

Start with non-controversial, easy questions. Don't worry about periods of silence. Give the person time to think.

Follow up on answers in order to find out "how" and "why."

Be flexible. If you are getting interesting information, don't be afraid to go on into a topic you hadn't planned in your outline of questions.

---

[3]Based on "Doing an Interview," Minnesota Community Studies Project, 1977; *Oral History* by Willa K. Baum, American Association for State and Local History, 1971; and *An Inquirer's Handbook,* Education Development Center, Inc., 1975.

STATE HISTORY AND COMMUNITY STUDY

Be a good listener.

Don't talk too much.

Don't give your opinions.

Don't go too long. An hour is probably the maximum time for an interview.

C. **Then What?**

After the interview, thank the person for his or her cooperation. Visit with the person and find out how he or she felt about the interview.

Write up a summary of your interview as soon as possible. Use the words of the person you interviewed whenever possible.

Other Ways of Encountering the Past

Sample pages from mail order catalogs from the past can initiate work in social history. Reproductions of a variety of catalogs are commercially available. Copies of these and others are often held in the collections of public libraries and historical societies. Groups of students can examine pages to formulate questions that can be answered by people who were living when the catalog was current. Pages dealing with toys, children's clothing, furniture, and appliances are especially effective. Students who have access to appropriate people are usually eager to take the sample pages and questions to them.

Discussion of items in the catalog can be extended to include a variety of artifacts — a tool for shelling corn, cooking utensils, a blade for trimming horses' hooves. These items can be borrowed from local historical societies for students to puzzle over, hypothesize about, and actively research. Artifacts encourage students to become involved with other sources of information that will verify hunches and extend knowledge about use of the item being considered.

Usually, the teacher needs to find only one intriguing object, and students will take up the challenge to find others — encouraging classmates to guess, then explaining their own knowledge of the gadget, and making clear where they got the information.

There are many other activities which teachers can devise for individual student projects. *Doing History* (Beery, 1984) is a recent adaptation of the Minnesota Community Studies approaches. It includes a series of "Do It Ideas" to guide students in specific community and personal history activities. These activities usually require the teacher's guidance at various steps. Figure 2 reproduces "Do It Idea #1," which asks students to find out what was happening in the nation and the world when they were born. They reseach events and trends in popular culture as well as in politics. Through these activities, students learn historical information and become accustomed to using source materials.

What was happening when *you* were born? Find and report:
- important news that month
- movies, TV shows, and popular songs of the time
- clothing styles of the time

FIND OUT
1. Check at the local newspaper office for copies of local papers for the week you were born.
2. Check the library for old magazines such as *Newsweek, Time,* and *Life.*
3. Check with your parents.

Figure 2. "Do It Sheet" is a starter for *Doing History.*

Evaluating Sources of Information

It is important that young people learn to evaluate their sources of information. This is especially true when students are collecting interview data. The following set of questions was intended for use by high school students. Regardless of age level, these kinds of criteria need to be introduced carefully, with a variety of examples drawn from the student's experiences.

IS THAT THE TRUTH?

How do you know that the information you collect is accurate? Do you believe everything you hear? Do your sources deliberately distort the truth? Do they unconsciously distort the truth?

These are the kinds of questions people who do history must consider all of the time. This is a particularly serious problem when you gather your information through interviews. People forget. They tell you only some of the things they know.

The following questions may help you decide whether the person you talked to was a good source of information.

Closeness
1. Did this person actually *see* or *live* the experiences described? Or is this person just telling about what he or she has heard from someone else?
2. How much time passed between the event and the time when it was written or told? Do you think this "time-gap" affected the accuracy of the information?

Competence
1. Does the person have special training or experience that would help make him or her an especially good observer — an "authority" or "expert"?
2. Was the person old enough and knowledgeable enough to understand what was happening?
3. Was the person deliberately watching and studying the event, or was he or she just there at the time?
4. If the person draws conclusions or makes a value judgment about a happening, do the facts he or she gives support this conclusion or judgment?
5. If you can check what one person tells you with other sources on a topic, do these sources agree?

Bias
1. What is this person's point of view about the past? (Does he or she remember only the "good old days," or does he or she always talk about "how awful it was"?)
2. How do you think this point of view affects the person's memory?
3. How do you think this point of view may affect what the person deliberately avoids talking about? (Is there any mention of deaths in the family? Are known conflicts among members of the family ever discussed?)
4. Do you think he or she may have exaggerated or stretched the truth to get a laugh or to make the story more exciting?
5. Is the person trying to create or protect a particular kind of image? How do you think that affects what he or she tells you?
6. Does the person seem to have a good memory?
7. Did the person express any strong feelings or prejudices that might have affected his or her memory?

In Conclusion

Admittedly, both of these approaches to state history — through community case studies and activities in family and local history — will result in fragmentary coverage of the substance of state history. When the many skills involved are taught and carefully practiced, there will be little or no time left for the standard survey. On the other hand, students who are exposed to these innovative approaches will be more likely to develop skills, perspectives, concepts, and enthusiasms that can stimulate further learning about the past. How can teachers become more comfortable with this trade-off? The following suggestions may help:

• Approach the geography of the state through map study, using official state road maps, if available. This study can use lively worksheets to teach practical map-reading skills, as well as to pinpoint key features and places in the state. Have students plan routes and calculate mileage from their community to communities they will study. Also, in states where it is appropriate, have students locate existing Indian reservations.

• A time line is often useful as a way to fill in gaps in history left by the case studies. Detailed time lines — including details not thoroughly developed in

class study — are seldom useful. They do not result in understanding, but merely confuse and stifle interest. A simple, uncluttered time line that orders the case materials can contribute to understanding.
- Use current news of state and local elections, annual township meetings, biennial political caucuses, and legislative sessions to teach the structure and functions of state of local government. Ongoing contacts with a local legislator to follow a piece of significant local legislation can be of special value.

Additional sources of concrete, lively family and community history activities include:
- Dennis J. Thavenet, "Family History: Coming Face-to-Face with the Past." How To Do It Series 2, No. 15. Washington: National Council for the Social Studies, 1981.
- R. Beery. *Doing History,* 615 S.W. 7th Street, Rochester, Minnesota 55902, Independent School District 535, 1984.
- Fay D. Metcalf and Matthew T. Downey. *Using History in the Classroom.* Nashville: The American Association for State and Local History, 1982.
- Thad Sitton, George L. Mehaffy, and O. L. Davis, Jr. *Oral History: A Guide for Teachers (and Others).* Austin: University of Texas Press, 1983.
- David Weitzman. *My Backyard History Book.* Boston: Little, Brown and Company, 1975.
- The Chicago Neighborhood History Project, 60 West Walton Street, Chicago, Illinois 60610.

CHAPTER V / TERRY ZELLER

Using the Visual Arts to Interpret the Community

American schools have traditionally been concerned with teaching young people to read, write, compute, and become active and responsible citizens of our democratic republic. Recently, the technological explosion and changes in the workplace have spurred efforts to make students "computer literate" and able to function in our fast-paced, machine-oriented society. For the most part, formal and informal education is word-centered. We learn from the written word, spoken word, and, more recently, the recorded word, transmitted on films, television sets, and computers.

Frequently, when films or pictures or television programs are presented, we are asked only to look, not to *see*. Our attention is focused for us. We are directed by the media and do not have to survey the image on our own to draw meaning from it. It is often thought that where there is an eye, there is also perception. However, this is not necessarily true. Visual acuity can and should be taught as a basic skill. However, teachers rarely instruct their students how to "read" a painting, building, or other artifact. Even the most cursory survey of social studies textbooks will make it apparent that pictures are often merely a "window dressing"; rarely is the student asked to draw information or concepts from the image itself. Captions to these illustrations tend to be merely explanatory or descriptive; usually, no effort is made to help the student analyze visual data and relate them in a meaningful way to the text.

Formal instruction in learning to look at objects can be a major strategy for teaching students to select, discriminate, analyze, categorize, and synthesize. Along with learning how to read maps, decipher statistical data, and interpret charts and graphs, students need to receive formal instruction in visual perception in order to help them to understand their natural and built environments.

A great deal of valuable information about the community is not buried in history books or in the written records of newspapers, businesses, or governments, but instead is displayed on the walls of art museums and historical societies, in paintings, photographs, prints, and drawings. Murals on the outside walls of buildings also have stories to tell, as do houses on country lanes and buildings on city streets. Both the "roots" — the historical life of a community — and its changing and varied faces are recorded in the artifacts of the community. The visual arts of a community also help to document the fact that history does not occur uniformly. Standard periodization of national history is not directly translatable to the local level. National centers of power, taste, and influence, such as, Washington, New York, Los Angeles, and Boston, influence local communities in very different ways. National trends and events are filtered through local customs and outlook and take on unique qualities peculiar to the individual community.

This chapter will explore ways in which the visual arts can be utilized in teaching about both urban and rural communities. Specific programs in various parts of the country will be cited, and teaching suggestions will be made using selected visual arts material from a variety of communities in different geographical locations. The visual arts will be construed in a broad sense to include everything from easel painting to domestic architecture.

In a society as homogeneous and standardized as ours has become, visual arts provide valuable evidence of a community's roots before the day when mass transportation, mass communication, and mass production began to erode regional and local distinctions. The visual documents of a community speak to us not only about origins, but also about those factors that, under the surface of Seven-Eleven Stores, designer jeans, Big Macs, network television, and syndicated newspaper columns and cartoons, make a community unique and vital.

Paintings and the Past

Landscapes, cityscapes, and genre scenes of the community or region are not only visual records of the natural and built environment of a particular time; they also document the values and social customs of the day — how people dressed, how they decorated their homes, how they made social status or social class clear for all to see, how they earned a living, and how they spent their leisure time. Paintings tell us something of the prevailing taste and aesthetic outlook of a community at a particular point in time. Reflecting upon the events, people, and activities that did not get painted can tell us as much about a community as those that have been preserved for posterity in paint or pencil.

The frequency with which Niagara Falls was painted during the late eighteenth and early nineteenth centuries reflects the sense of pride and wonder that this natural phenomenon inspired in Americans, who, because they had no ancient temples or castles to be monuments to the nation's greatness, turned to the fabulous natural richness and glory of the nation. In time, American artists like Albert Bierstadt and Thomas Moran would transform the Rocky Mountains, Yosemite, and the Grand Canyon into icons of American greatness. On a somewhat smaller scale, landscape paintings of subjects such as the Falls of St. Anthony and Minnehaha Falls in Minnesota served a didactic and patriotic purpose in nineteenth-century America. Such works not only document American geography and westward expansion, and, in instances where Native Americans appear, ethnicity; they also speak of American values and nationalism. Many county historical societies are rich in such visual documentation of a community's or region's frontier appearance. The Winona County (Minnesota) Historical Society, for example, has a number of nineteenth-century paintings of public buildings and commercial structures that have survived to the present, albeit altered in form or function.

Portraits, in addition to recording hair styles, fashions in clothing, and sometimes interior decorative arts, are mirrors held up to a community's leading citizens, and, as such, tell us something of the life and values of the community. In the Colonial South, it was the planter class who had their portraits painted. In Boston in the same period, John Singleton Copley was painting the merchants and artisans of that busy commercial and manufacturing community. Copley's portraits of Paul Revere and Nathaniel Hurd document the appearance, culture, and socioeconomic make-up of Boston society in the 1760s. Likewise, the many portraits of Puritan ministers located in museums at Yale and in Worcester, as well as the Brookline Historical Society, and the Wadsworth Athenaeum, are visual testimony to the power of Calvinist theology that played such an important part in the life of countless New England communities, helping to shape behavior as well as the physical layout and institutions of those towns. Students of these communities would do well to study these early portraits.

The Baltimore Museum of Art, the Peale Museum, and the Maryland Historical Society all contain important paintings of the city of Baltimore and the state's leading colonial families, such as the Calverts, as well as locally prominent men of business and public service. Local museums and county historical societies often contain portraits of local worthies. The Lancaster County Historical Society in Pennsylvania has portraits of nineteenth-century Lancaster's "first citizens" by such artists as Jacob Eichholtz and Arthur Armstrong, while the St. Louis County Historical Society (Duluth, Minnesota) has portraits and landscapes by such well-known artists of the last century as Eastman Johnson. The Le Sueur County Historical Society, also in Minnesota, collects and exhibits works by Minnesota artists. The same is true of scores of historical societies and art and heritage centers across the nation.

Public Art

Public art refers to those aesthetic works one finds out of doors, such as buildings, statues, wall murals, and even gravestones. What can be learned in a cemetery about a community's past is not limited to the writing on the headstones. The style, craftmanship, and subject matter (iconography) of gravestones tell us something of the values and religious beliefs held in the community over time. What, for example, does the progression in imagery from a winged skull, to a smiling angelic face, to a classical urn, to a mourning figure under a weeping willow reveal about changing values and outlook? The architecture of a community can indicate settlement patterns, the availability of building materials and necessary technology, ethnicity, the balance between aesthetic consciousness and practical considerations, socioeconomic levels, and the degree to which regional, national, and international influences have affected the community.

The Hedwig Hill double log cabin, at the Ranching Heritage Center in Lubbock, Texas (Fig. 1), not only reflects the adaptation of shelter to the climate and environment of the Texas Hill Country, but also mirrors the available technology and building techniques of nineteenth-century German immigrants. German immigrants to Texas in the nineteenth century were among the most skilled builders of log structures on the frontier. In the Texas Hill Country in and around Fredericksburg and San Antonio, structures similar to the Hedwig Hill House are tangible evidence of the adaptability of German building techniques to local conditions. Such double log cabins, with a covered breezeway, or dogtrot, connecting them, were common sights in this part of Texas in the middle years of the last century. They were situated so as to take advantage of the prevailing breeze to cool the house during the long warm season. The family generally lived on the dogtrot during hot weather, cooking, eating, and sleeping there. With locally available post oak and cedar, these settlers built their houses, most frequently using a V-notch to hold the logs in place. Such V-shaped joints or notches are also found in early log buildings in areas of Pennsylvania settled by Germans. Wide spaces between the logs filled with rock-and-mud chinking to keep out the elements were also typical of German log construction techniques. Thus, the ethnic origins of settlers of the rural Texas Hill Country can be established in part from architectural remains.

A fully developed unit or lesson on a community using vernacular domestic architecture would also involve an analysis of the uses of interior space and styles of interior decoration. Vernacular architecture refers to styles which originate in the communities in which they are used. Study of vernacular architecture can focus on such questions as:

- Were the rooms single- or multi-purpose?
- Which rooms are "public" space; which are clearly private? How can you tell the difference?
- How have the inhabitants of the house attempted to personalize its rooms?
- Where does the family gather in the house?

The functions of rooms in a house have changed over time as the nature of the family has changed, as sex roles have changed, and as technology has exerted its influence. Patterns of use also differ to some degree according to the ethnic origin, socioeconomic level, and employment of members of the family. Information about these important factors in the make-up of the basic

Figure 1. Hedwig Log Cabin

Figure 2. George Hastings Law Office

unit of the community — the household — is visually evident in the historic house museums and period room settings of museums.

While the Hedwig Hill House illustrates vernacular architecture, the Hastings law Office at Genesee Country Museum (Fig. 2) illustrates the revival of a classical style of architecture. This style of architecture, based on that of ancient Greece, was used from about 1820 to 1840 and became a part of the lives of the people in many parts of America. Another example of how local communities adapt an academic or formal style of architecture to parochial needs is seen in many of the cottages at the Landisville Camp Meeting Grounds in Landisville, Pennsylvania (Fig. 3). These cottages tell both of the local revival of the Gothic (medieval) style in domestic architecture and of the traditional association in the popular mind of religion with the pointed arch windows and other typical Gothic features. The Landisville Camp Meeting Grounds in conservative Lancaster County has been the scene of evangelical revival meetings since the late nineteenth century.

Large sections of Lancaster County, Pennsylvania, were settled by German immigrants, many of whom were seeking freedom from religious persecution in Europe. Among these were the Mennonites and the Amish. Early Mennonite settlers — such as Hans Herr, who built a house in southern Lancaster County in 1719 — constructed their new world homes in much the same manner as the buildings they had known in the old world. The Hans Herr House (Fig. 4) served as both a home and a Mennonite meeting house. While built of local sandstone, it looks exactly like a medieval house that one might find in a south German city such as Heidelberg or Nuernberg. The gabled roof, large central fireplace, small casement windows, and asymmetrical arrangement of the door and windows all document a strong medieval German influence. The skill with which the dressed stone was laid clearly tells us that an expert stone mason was locally available and had the tools necessary to do so fine a job of construction.

We see a similar medieval tradition, this time executed in wood, in the architectural style of The Cloister in Ephrata, also in Lancaster County, Pennsylvania. This religious community, related to the German Pietist movement, was founded in 1732, by Johann Conrad Beissel, who was driven from Germany because of his religious beliefs. The followers of Beissel lived and worked communally. Some lived in family units, while others led celibate lives in dormitory-like buildings (Fig. 5) — the men in the Saal (House of Prayer, left, 1741), and the women in the Saron (Sister's House, right, 1743).

Beissel's faithful, the Mennonites, and the Amish — the latter often referred to as "Plain People" — lived austere lives and held to their simple forms of worship. Although the Ephrata community was dissolved in the mid-1930s, Lancaster County today still has a sizable population of other "Plain" sects. We can gain a deeper appreciation of their present-day life styles and beliefs by studying the sturdy, functional houses and furniture, such as the kasses (wardrobes or chests) that they built during the eighteenth century.

Baltimore, Maryland, is famous for its row houses, some dating back to Georgian-style town houses of the eighteenth century. The row house is an important material document in the life of this community. A walking or bus tour of the city reveals how this type of domestic structure has evolved over the years, both shaping life for Baltimorians and being shaped by them to fit their changing needs and changes in technology and aesthetic tastes. Baltimore is making a concerted and impressively successful effort to preserve the past through restoration and adaptive use of old buildings. This story can be read

VISUAL ARTS TO INTERPRET COMMUNITY 63

Figure 3. Landisville Camp Meeting Grounds, Landisville, Pennsylvania

Lancaster Mennonite Conference Historical Society

Figure 4. Hans Herr House

Figure 5. Ephrata Cloister

Figure 6. Row Houses, Baltimore, Maryland

visually in neighborhood after neighborhood where eighteenth-century row houses stand side by side with new construction designed to blend with the old (Fig. 6).

Historical photographs that students find at home, in the public library, or at the local historical society can help to recreate the fabric of the community's past. Buildings that have disappeared are as important in telling the story of the community as those that remain. Consideration of the way a site has been used when a building was torn down and the type and style of structure that replaced it helps to document changes in the socioeconomic life, values, and land use of the community. One can gain research skills through analysis of historical photographs. The subjects which people chose to photograph tell us not only about the local pastimes, but also about clothing styles and locally important buildings and landmarks, as well as what scenes people thought picturesque or interesting and worth preserving. Examining old photographs helps us understand the values and tastes of certain members of the community at a given point in time.

Many communities have statues or monuments in their parks or town squares. The persons whom the community chooses to honor with such monuments, together with the style and manner of the presentations, reveal important information about the history and values of that particular community. The pioneer memorial (Fig. 8) in Lubbock, Texas, tells us that this community values the frontier experiences of families who won a living from the land by hard work, self-discipline, sacrifice, and determination. The pioneer dress of the nineteenth century, the hoe with "the land" sticking to it in places and the mother with her flower and Bible are all emblematic of values

Figure 7. West Texas Farm Family

which the people of West Texas treasure. For all of the detailed realism of the execution, the monument remains an idealization of the community's values as expressed in a bronze plaque near the base of the statue, which reads:

The first settlers in West Texas were cattle drovers ... later on the farmers came with their families, to plow the land and to build homes. These settlers brought culture, religion, and education. They built schools and churches and endured many hardships because of their determination, honesty, and integrity. We in West Texas today enjoy the rich heritage they left behind.

Figure 8. West Texas Pioneer Family Memorial

But by comparing this sculpture with a nineteenth-century photograph of a West Texas pioneer family (Fig. 7) we can understand how historical fact becomes historical myth. The photograph does not idealize the frontier experience as the statue does.

Statues and monuments are not the only artistic testimonials to a community's heritage and values. Beginning in the 1960s, public art began to appear on the blank walls of stores, warehouses, and other public buildings across the nation. This art reflected efforts to engage local people in revitalizing their inner-city neighborhoods. Wall murals on buildings in St. Paul, Minnesota — one in a Native American neighborhood (Fig. 9) and another in a Hispanic section of the city (Fig. 10) — are visual evidence of a large urban Indian population in the Twin Cities and a concentration of Hispanic Americans proud of their pre-Columbian heritage. These works express ethnic pride in simple, strong, realistic forms and symbols.

Figure 9. Mural, St. Paul, Minnesota

Figure 10. Mural, St. Paul, Minnesota

Ideas for Teaching

In using the arts for teaching about the community, one should identify those aspects of a community's past and present that might be documented visually. Teachers might search out images that record particular events in the community's history. For example, teachers who are presenting the Great Depression, the Dust Bowl years, and the New Deal might discover that a community-based unit on the New Deal would be very effective. A part of this unit could involve an investigation of local WPA projects. One project, for example, might include an investigation of local art deco buildings that were built as WPA projects.

The story of the plight of the Okies can take on new dimensions and have great impact on students if they are able to visit such local visual arts institutions as the Gilcrease Museum and the Philbrook Art Center, both in Tulsa, Oklahoma, to examine the paintings of artists working during the 1930s. Alexander Hogue's *Mother Earth Laid Bare* (Fig. 11) is a particularly compelling example. Between the rusting plow and pools of run-off rain water in the foreground and the broken barbed wire fence, abandoned farm buildings, and dead tree in the background, a naked Mother Earth lies prostrate, vulnerable, and, by implication, raped. Hogue's works are powerful statements about land use, ecology, and the history of the Plains states in the 1930s. Important insights into the history of many western American communites can be gained by

Figure 11. Alexandre Hogue. Erosion No. 2: Mother Earth Laid Bare

examining such paintings in conjunction with photographs of migrant families, farmers, and bread lines taken as part of a New Deal project administered by the Farm Security Administration.

During the years 1934 to 1943, the WPA, under its Federal Art Project, paid artists to paint murals for public buildings all over the United States. Many of these were done for small town and rural post offices, from Kennebunkport, Maine, to Pacific Grove, California. These WPA murals document small town and rural America. They include a mural entitled *Cheese Making* in the United States Post Office in Plymouth, Wisconsin; another entitled *Band Concert* in Corning, Iowa; an Iroquois Indian panel in the United States Post Office in Honeoye Falls, New York; and a mural entitled *Youth* in the United States Post Office in Atlantic City, New Jersey, showing the famous oceanfront resort. For the most part, the murals render American scenes in a realistic style, though some tend in the direction of simplification of form or abstraction.

Local committees had a considerable voice in determining the subject matter and even the execution of the murals. This local influence contributed at times to a high degree of idealization. The mural in the United States Post Office in Paris, Arkansas, entitled *Rural Arkansas* (Fig. 12), painted by Joseph P. Vorst, is a good case in point. The up-to-date stock farm in the left foreground, the freshly painted, well-kept buildings and fences, and the clean, unpatched clothes of the workers — including the black field hands — presents an

Figure 12. Joseph P. Vorst. Rural Arkansas USPO, Paris, Arkansas

idealized image of the rural South in the 1930s that is inconsistent with the picture that one gets from photographs taken by James Agee and Walker Evans for the Farm Security Administration and published in *Let Us Now Praise Famous Men.* Nor is it the same rural South described in the local interviews conducted by the WPA Federal Writers' Project or in Erskine Caldwell's novels *God's Little Acre* and *Tobacco Road.* Thus, these WPA murals are valuable not only for what they tell us about local economy and life, but also as documents of a community's values, aspirations, and view of itself at a particular time. A variety of social studies projects could center on these visual arts documents. An important resource for study of the WPA murals is a recent book by Karal Ann Marling, entitled *Wall-to-Wall America: A Cultural History of Post Office Murals in the Great Depression,* published by the University of Minnesota Press.

Some county historical societies are using the work of local artists to interpret their community. In Walker, Minnesota, the Ah-Gwah-Ching Historical Society has exhibited paintings and prints in its collection by Minnesota artists who produced works on local themes as part of the WPA's Federal Art Project. An updated version of the WPA program, the CETA-financed Mendocino County (California) Murals in Public Places Project used six local artists to paint murals in public buildings in the town of Ukiah. These murals feature historical scenes depicting the development of local industries such as fishing, ranching, and lumbering, as well as one in the court house illustrating the Pomo Indians' story of creation. They, like the surviving WPA murals, are valuable aesthetic records of their community's past.

A unit or lesson on the community's built environment might focus on local architecture. Government records, place and street names, street maps, and city phone directories, as well as local histories and historical photographs or paintings, could provide information on the community's development.

Virtually every community contains one or more structures of historical or architectural importance. Such buildings can reveal much about a community's past. From studying architecture we can learn something of a commu-

VISUAL ARTS TO INTERPRET COMMUNITY 69

Figure 13. Henry Lewis. St. Anthony Falls, 1855.

Figure 14. Ferdinand Reichardt. St. Anthony Falls, 1857.

Figure 15. Peter G. Clausen. Reconstructing St. Anthony Falls

Figure 16. Alexis Fournier. St. Anthony Falls and Suspension Bridge, 1884.

nity's roots and how the community has changed over time. Using the built environment as a base for studying the community can involve students in in-depth learning about their home town or rural area. A visual survey of the community supplemented by research into old city maps, newspapers, photographs, tax records, local zoning ordinances, and telephone and commercial directories can reveal changing patterns of land use.

In some communities, organized study of the built environment is already under way. In Texas, the Beaumont Heritage Society and the Beaumont Art Museum in 1979–80 initiated an eighth-grade program entitled, "Beaumont USA: Our Built Environment," intended to help public and private school students to develop an awareness of their architectural environment. The seventeen-week unit uses role-playing, hands on historic preservation activities, and contact with architects and other community resource people to teach basic cognitive skills such as observation, analysis, synthesis, and evaluation. In studying about historical buildings, students learn to draw information from such varied sources as oral histories, public and private written documents, and, most important of all, the structures themselves. Analysis of changes in building materials, techniques of construction, designs, ornamentation, usage, and the immediate natural and built environment makes students aware of how the social, economic, ethnic and value systems of their community have altered over time.

At the Massie School in Savannah, Georgia, a "Heritage Classroom Program" for students in grades 4–12 is an enrichment project involving the careful study of a number of historical structures in the city.

The Corcoran Gallery of Art in Washington, DC, has developed an impressive instructional unit, "Architecture Is Elementary," which focuses on teaching about architecture as an art form. A number of the instructional strategies used in the Corcoran materials could be adapted to the needs of social studies teachers who are preparing community study units involving the built environment.

Structured and focused study of the built environment not only teaches problem solving, critical thinking, and other basic skills, but can also bring students into contact with resource people from the community who may acquaint them with career possibilities. More importantly, study of the built environment will help to instill civic pride and a desire to preserve what is unique and beautiful in the community.

Another approach to studying the community through the visual arts is to examine paintings of the town or area at different periods in its history to identify themes or subjects that shed light upon the community's past and present. For example, we can document technological and economic development in Minneapolis, Minnesota, through paintings. In Henry Lewis's *St. Anthony Falls As It Appeared in 1843* (Fig. 13), we can see an Indian, like Rousseau's noble savage—a "child of nature"—sitting and contemplating the untamed natural beauty of the Falls of St. Anthony. Along the banks of the Mississippi here at these falls, the city of Minneapolis was to grow from the tiny community of St. Anthony. Early settlers of Minneapolis continued to draw upon the hydropower of the falls to build the city into a center of lumbering and milling. Ferdinand Reichardt's *St. Anthony Falls* (Fig. 14) shows the powerful cataract less than ten years after Lewis' painting. Already a bridge spans the torrent and mills along the bank use its energy to process the raw materials of the region. Smoke no longer rises from a contemplative Indian's pipe, but from stacks on a mill's roof. The Winslow House Hotel is seen on the hill in the distance. When Peter Clausen painted his *St. Anthony Falls: Break in the Tunnel, No. 1* in 1869 (Fig. 15), industrialization had resulted in the ecological damage which he depicts. Factories and mills now form a solid front along the river bank and the twin towers of an improved wooden suspension bridge can be seen in the distance, along with smokey factory stacks. The artist Alexis Fournier, a native of St. Paul, took Minneapolis, and the river front in particular, as his subject on a number of occasions, giving us wonderful visual documents of Minneapolis in the 1880s. His peaceful sunset scene of the river (Fig. 16) shows us the still tiny village of St. Anthony on the right bank across the river from the more recent and now burgeoning city of Minneapolis, the smoke from whose factories and mills blends in a non-threatening way with the clouds at sunset. The painting can be dated by the buildings along the bank and the wooden suspension bridge in the distance, and by the absence of the stone arch bridge that James J. Hill, the St. Paul railroad baron, was to build across the river at this point some years later. By the time Arnold Klagstad painted his *Three Bridges* in 1937 (Fig. 17), the Minneapolis side of the Mississippi had changed again. The streamlined "art deco" train on the old stone arched bridge in the middle distance tells of technological progress since Fournier painted the Minneapolis skyline.

That artists would take the Mississippi at St. Anthony Falls as their subject for nearly a century is a measure of both the interest in the natural phenomenon and the fascination with the industrialization of America. Teaching activities using these paintings of Minneapolis would involve identifying specific structures like the famous Winslow House Hotel in Reichardt's painting, the suspension bridge in Clausen's and Fournier's paintings, and the stone arch bridge in the Klagstad painting. Students could then try to locate them in the city today.

Teachers might ask students to answer the following questions: If these structures have disappeared, what has replaced them? Can you identify in *Three Bridges* the building in the left background with the tall tower? When was it built? What was its function? Was it "up-to-date" in style when it was built? Would it look "out of place" in the twentieth-century? How has the architecture of Minneapolis changed from the time Reichardt painted *Saint Anthony Falls* to the time Klagstad painted *Three Bridges*? What do the choice and treatment of subject matter in these paintings tell us about nineteenth century attitudes toward industrialization and technology?

One might well try to locate the exact places along the river depicted by

Figure 17. Arnold Klagstad. Three Bridges, 1937.

Fournier and others to compare and contrast those scenes in the past and present. How has the use of the river front changed from the 1850s to the 1980s? What about the Minneapolis skyline might attract artists today?

Clearly, the city grew up and was regulated by the pulse and power of the river. Has the center of metropolitan life shifted away from the river by the 1980s? If so, why? How do these paintings document some of the damage done to the natural environment by material and technological progress? How do these paintings help us to understand the community of Minneapolis?

Some Conclusions

Using the visual arts to interpret the community means getting out of the classroom and away from the traditional textbook approach to social studies. The community is a vast learning resource, rich in visual documents of the life, work, play, and values of the people — past and present — who live there. By utilizing the visual arts in teaching about the community, one will broaden and deepen the content of the social studies curriculum, reinforce the development of basic skills, and help make students aware of the importance of the physical environment and quality of life in their community.

Using the approach to instruction described in this chapter is not easy. It involves a great deal of nontraditional teacher preparation, and draws the social studies teacher into subjects which may be unfamiliar, such as architecture, art history, and American Studies. A short selected bibliography of resources is provided here to familiarize teachers with some of the basic literature and methods useful in teaching about the community through the visual arts.

Bibliography

Alcock, N. "Vernacular Architecture: Historical Evidence and Historical Problems," in *Material Culture and the Study of American Life,* Ian M. G. Quimby (ed.).New York: W. W. Norton and Company, Inc., 1978, 109–120.

Andrews, W. *Architecture, Ambition and Americans: A Social History of American Architecture.* New York: Free Press, 1964.

Barker, C. "History Hikes: How to Put History in Your Walking Tour," *History News,* April 1981, 10–11.

Beckow, S. M. "Culture, History, and Artifact," in *Material Culture Studies in America,* Thomas J. Schlereth (ed.). Nashville: The American Association for State and Local History, 1982, 114–123.

Carson, C. "Doing History with Material Culture," in *Material Culture and the Study of American Life,* Ian M. G. Quimby (ed.). New York: W. W. Norton and Company, Inc. 1978, 41–64.

Chittenden, V. A. "Folk Art: Is It Art? Is It Folk? Is It History?" *History News,* June 1982, 13–16.

Craig, T. L. "Aesthetics Aside: How to Find Historical Information in Works of Art," *History News,* June 1982, 17–19.

Ellsworth, L., and Ellsworth, L.V. "House-Reading: How to Study Historic Houses as Symbols of Society," *History News,* May 1980, 9–13.

Foley, M. M. *The American House.* New York: Harper and Row Publishers, 1980.

Gowans, A. *Images of American Living.* New York: Harper and Row Publishers, 1976.

Handlin, D. P. *The American Home: Architecture and Society, 1815–1915.* Boston: Little, Brown, and Company, 1979.

Hobbs, J. A. *Art in Context.* New York: Harcourt Brace Jovanovich, Inc., 1975.

Holt, G. E. "Chicago Through a Camera Lens: An Essay on Photography as History," in *Material Culture Studies in America,* Thomas J. Schlereth (ed.). Nashville: The American Association for State and Local History, 1982, 178–288.

Lange, L. "Learning To Care: How Beaumont, Texas Teaches Kids to Care About the Built Environment," *History News,* July 1980, 13–15.

Larkin, O. W. *Art and Life in America.* New York: Rinehart and Company, Inc. 1950.

Lohof, B. A. "The Service Station in America: The Evolution of a Vernacular Form," in *Material Culture Studies in America,* Thomas J. Schlereth (ed.). Nashville: The American Association for State and Local History, 1982, 251–258.

Mumford, L. *Sticks and Stones: A Study of American Architecture and Civilization,* 2nd ed., New York: Dover Publications, 1955.

O'Sullivan, T. "Art and History: Regional Art Enhances Local History Programs," *History News,* June 1982, 10–12.

Schlereth, T.J. "Historic Houses As Learning Laboratories: Seven Teaching Strategies." Technical Leaflet No. 105. Nashville: The American Association for State and Local History, 1978.

Schroeder, F.E.H. "Schoolhouse Reading: What You Can Learn from Your Rural School." *History News,* April 1981, 15–16.

Taylor, J. *America As Art.* New York: Harper and Row, Publishers, 1976.

CHAPTER VI / R. BEERY AND ROBERT J. TODD

Citizenship Grounded in Community

It is fashionable to express alarm over levels of voter participation. There is consternation that a president may be thought to have a clear mandate to reshape the federal government on the strength of the ballots cast by little more than one-fourth of the nation's eligible voters. Schools — and social studies programs in particular — often come under fire because of the low turnout of young voters.

This focus on voting reflects a view of democracy as a system where "the people" freely choose those who govern. Voting for preferred candidates is emphasized as basic. When people do not vote, democratic institutions are considered to be in danger, because they can be controlled by interests cynically bent on exploiting society. This emphasis on voting can obscure a fuller, more complete perspective on citizenship in a potentially democratic society.

Decision-making and government in an open society need to be based on a variety of citizen involvements. Consequently, it is necessary that a full range of participation skills and strategies be taught and that the values which support these modes of civic participation be fostered. Responsible citizenship requires individual skills to maintain and strengthen the democratic practices that enhance liberty. Participation skills need to be grounded in commitments to individual freedom and rational thought. These commitments should guide the shaping of political party positions at the "grassroots" level, the formation of neighborhood associations, the active pursuit of quality service by local government, and many other activities directly or indirectly related to public policies and governance.

Emerging Ideas

Daniel Yankelovich (1981) emphasizes a decided shift away from "self denial" to an active, often restless search for "self-fulfillment." In exploring the dimensions of this change, Yankelovich asserts, "Perhaps the sharpest shift in American attitudes has been a steady erosion of trust in government and other institutions" (p. 184). In reviewing key research, Yankelovich concludes that "in the course of a single generation Americans have grown disillusioned about the relation of the American to his government" (p.185). Yankelovich also contends that individuals are increasingly insistent that the quality of their own lives be improved.

Analyzing the "megatrends" that are "transforming our lives," John Naisbitt (1982) considers these changes in a different light. He sees a shift away from traditional representative democracy to dynamic participatory democracy and a movement toward decentralization. Naisbitt concludes that there has been "a huge upsurge in grassroots political activity everywhere in the United States" (p. 113). He argues that centralized solutions to problems are ineffective, asserting that "Successful initiatives hammered out at the local level have staying power. Local solutions are resistant to top-down intervention and become models for others still grappling with the problems" (p. 112).

Whether or not one agrees with the observations of Yankelovich or Naisbitt, the desirability of involving high school students in community-based political and governmental experiences cannot be denied. Young people can benefit enormously from an opportunity to apply skills developed in their government courses and to expand their knowledge through real world contacts. Because of the immediacy and pervasiveness of local life, and because it is the context in which young people experience and perceive civic activity, increased attention should be given to participation at the local level.

Developmental Needs

Special attention should be given to the unique developmental needs and capabilities of youngsters between the ages of nine and thirteen. It is during these years that many students begin to develop the concepts and skills required for political participation. It is also during these years that youngsters become capable of undertaking specific activities, and roles that help to clarify their ideas of government. One summary of research on political learning (Dawson et al., 1977), notes:

> Changes in political perceptions between the early childhood period and the end of late childhood are so great that for some scholars this is the most important period for political learning. By age ten or eleven children begin to move away from the highly personal and emotional perceptions and to comprehend more abstract ideas and relationships. Where younger children can do little more than identify political leaders, especially the president, as powerful and benevolent, older children show a greater capacity to understand and identify certain tasks that go along with particular political roles. During this period, information and cognitive content are added to the vague feelings and identifications acquired earlier. (p. 53–54)

School experiences are often designed to meet young children's needs for self-esteem. Social studies programs in primary grades focus upon expanding horizons of self, family, neighborhood, and community as supportive and responsive environments for children. Studying these helps young children to develop the highly positive loyalties and identities which prepare them for learning roles basic to responsible citizenship. However, between the primary school years and the ninth grade, when civics is generally taught, participatory citizenship education usually receives little attention. Social studies curricula frequently emphasize narrative history, descriptive geography, and comparative cultures in grades four through eight — precisely those years when students are capable of benefitting from systematic instruction that will stimulate growth of basic concepts, participatory skills, and personal commitments.

Developmental reseach indicates that by age fourteen or fifteen, most young people have already established basic perceptions, orientations, and commitments that will guide further learning and adult behavior. At the end of early childhood — at age eight or nine — children idealize government. The uniformity of positive attitudes is remarkable. During adolescence these positive attitudes generally begin to erode, and cynicism and alienation begin to take root in some. This pattern creates a need for carefully planned intervention during late childhood. Active learning experiences can help upper elementary students to see participation as valuable in their daily lives. Such experiences require teachers to focus on the life of the school and the community. First, students need to know what participation can involve; then they need to reflect on the benefits and costs of various forms of citizen participation.

Participation Skills

Schools should not prescribe a pattern of participation for "good citizenship." Citizenship involves developing and exercising participation skills that are grounded in a commitment to personal freedom and rational thought. Responsible citizenship requires individual participation to maintain and strengthen liberty. Ernest E. Bayles (1958) relates the notions of equality, participation, and responsibility in his observation that " . . . democracy should be defined as equality of opportunity to participate in making group decisions and equality of obligation to participate in carrying them out, once they are made and until they are revised or rescinded."

Particular skills are essential to the five participation roles identified by the American Political Science Association's High School Political Science Curriculum Project:

1. *Observers* are people who listen carefully to group discussion and watch a group carry out activities. It is necessary for some people to keep silent, watch group activity, and try to make helpful suggestions for future activities of the group.
2. *Supporters* are people who help to carry out an activity. They are good at helping others get things done. Without supporters, few groups could follow through on activities they plan.

3. *Advocates* are people who take sides on an issue and try to get others to agree with their positions. An advocate is a person who has a strong position on an issue and can state a position and reasons for that position.
4. *Facilitators* are people who try to help people understand other points of view and who aid the group in coming to a compromise on an issue. A facilitator listens to both sides and tries to reconcile differences of opinion to allow for a decision to be made.
5. *Organizers* are people who try to plan and put together group activities. An organizer is a leader. A person who can mobilize people behind a task and get things done in the group is an organizer (Gillespie and Lazarus, 1975).

Participation skills have been identified in various ways. The National Council for the Social Studies, in its statement on the Essentials of the Social Studies (1981), asserts that "Connecting the classroom with the community provides many opportunities for students to learn the basic skills of participation, from observation to advocacy." To learn these, the statement continues, the student needs to:

Work effectively in groups — organizing, planning, making decisions, taking action.
Form coalitions of interest with other groups.
Persuade, compromise, bargain.
Practice patience and perseverance in working for one's goal.
Develop experience in cross-cultural situations.

These elements of citizen involvement can be approached at every level.

Primary School, Hidden Curriculum, and Citizenship

In the early grades, participation which reinforces a commitment to human dignity, reason, and responsible action can lay a foundation for steadily maturing attitudes and behaviors. The "hidden curriculum" — the set of assumptions that structure personal and social life in the classroom and in the school — is perhaps the most important source of early notions about citizen behavior. Children's experiences in the classroom inevitably generate powerful ideas and feelings that will influence their attitudes toward the public world. Democratic behavior — the foundation of effective, responsible citizen participation — needs to permeate the child's initial experiences in classroom and school living. Carefully planned classroom activity that uses the hidden curriculum recognizes that patterns of interaction make major contributions to social learning and growth.

Children need to experience and practice democratic ideals before they encounter them as abstract principles in the formal curriculum. They need firsthand experience with:
- rights and responsibilities of individuals
- equality of opportunity
- due process
- consent of the governed

By discovering and applying these values in daily activities, young children can begin to understand the importance of participation in group decision-making. The sense that government is positive — that it is a set of "friendly helpers" eager to protect others — can be used as a springboard for showing young children how citizens perform their roles.

Patriotism is often a theme in commerical materials for the primary grades. The American flag, national heroes, national shrines, and other symbols are usually presented with arresting visuals and stirring narratives. While these do not ordinarily teach facts and abstract ideas about American civics, they arouse emotions which foster a lifelong commitment to being an American.

The local community is an excellent source of heroic persons, legends, and events that can be studied factually and concretely, as well as for their symbolic meaning. Buildings such as the county court house and the city hall are often inspirational to the young. Attention can also be focused on statues. Stories about the community's original Native American inhabitants and its immigrant settlers can be highlighted by reference to the actual locations of their acts. An account of the community's oldest building can be made more effective by a slide and comes to life if children are standing on that site. Walking tours are especially valuable in small towns.

When the helpful behavior of a neighborhood citizen is acclaimed and made a model, then children understand that commendable behavior is achievable in daily life. Teachers can focus attention on the teenaged candy striper, the older child who tutors in the classroom, the Girl Scout or Boy Scout troop leader, the person who voluntarily tends the flowers in front of the nursing home, and many others of all ages. In addition, worthy actions of class members should be acknowledged. Students might also discuss volunteer activities in which they have participated with their families.

Young children can be introduced very concretely to ways in which their neighbors and their own parents tackle local problems — working for a pet control ordinance, a stop light at a busy crossing, or a playground on a vacant lot. They can learn about elements of the political process as they witness the efforts of ordinary citizens to improve life through group action.

The Hidden Curriculum Beyond Primary School

It is important that individual participation in school and classroom life is emphasized and encouraged beyond the early years, on into the junior and senior high school experiences. Secondary schools tend to be more regimented, rule-bound, and openly coercive than smaller and less formal elementary schools. This fact should cause some concern, inasmuch as young people enter these schools at a time when they are developing more critical, distrustful, and even cynical attitudes toward authority. At times, the school's focus on control and obedience stimulates and reinforces this developmental phenomenon.

Secondary School Civics and Government

Secondary school government courses usually focus attention on national government, emphasizing institutional structure and functions. Study of the local community is seldom used to emphasize roles and participation processes in concrete terms. However, if the local environment is included, participation roles and citizenship competencies can be broadened and sharpened as they are applied to emerging issues. As students focus on those processes involved in being an observer, a supporter, an advocate, a facilitator, and an organizer on the local scene, they can gain a variety of experience using the seven citizenship competencies identified by Richard C. Remy: acquiring and using information, assessing involvement, making decisions, making judgments, communicating, cooperating, and promoting interests (Remy, n.d.). Such a framework of interrelated roles and skills provides a useful structure for teaching about the political process and government in the community.

There are several valuable sources of teaching ideas for involving secondary school students in community citizenship. Richard C. Remy's *Handbook of Basic Citizenship Competencies,* not only identifies the seven citizenship competencies specified above, but also includes valuable secondary school "sample learning experiences" related to specific competencies. A thorough approach to developing citizen competence is presented in *Education for Citizen Action — Challenge for Secondary Curriculum,* by Fred M. Newmann, and in *Skills in Citizen Action: An English-Social Studies Program for Secondary Schools,* by Fred M. Newmann, Thomas A. Bertocci, and Ruthanne M. Landsness.

The Northwest Regional Educational Laboratory's *Experienced-Based Learning: How To Make the Community Your Classroom* treats the entire community as a "learning environment," and delineates "functional citizenship" as a "life skill" (McClure et al., 1977). The following plan from that project asks students to consider the nature of government, their own roles in government, and ways in which they can be involved in social and political change.

CITIZENSHIP GROUNDED IN COMMUNITY

STARTER PROJECT: FUNCTIONAL CITIZENSHIP

Subject Title: My Role as a Citizen

Community Resources: Any adult citizens; any community site; government representative, either hired or elected; government agency, including Internal Revenue Service; state tax officials; county tax assessor; attorney; unions; personnel officers; agencies concerned with occupational safety and health; public interest research groups; employer associations.

School Resources: U.S. Constitution, government textbooks, newspapers and magazines, telephone directory.

Purpose: To become aware of the role of government in American life and how citizens can and should participate in governmental processes.

Suggested Activities:
1. Reasons for government
    a. Prepare a list of questions people often have about why government is or is not necessary.
    b. Using these questions, interview three adults in the community and record their answers.
    c. Write and discuss your own statement about why we have government. Be prepared to name categories of needs (society's and individual's) to which any government should respond, and be able to apply the categories in analyzing specific modes of government.
    d. Discuss with your community site resource person how decisions are made at that site. Compare this information with what other students may have discovered at their sites.
    e. Research your local government and report on:
        - The decision-making and responsibility structure
        - Making, interpreting, and enforcing laws
        - How citizens can affect decisions
    f. Discuss how you can make decisions for yourself in the following situations: at home, with friends, at community sites, at school. With whom do you share decision-making in each of these settings?

2. Citizen responsibility
    a. Select a social problem that concerns you. Investigate that problem as a concerned citizen and find out how you can help solve it using the following questions as a guide:
        - What is the problem? Who is affected by it?
        - What are the causes?
        - Who is trying to deal with the problem?
        - Is the government involved? How?
        - What are you going to do about it?
        - What must happen in order to solve the problem or improve the situation?
    b. Describe your plan of action in detail and secure staff approval before beginning your investigation.

3. American tax system
    a. At a privately owned business in the community, identify at least two kinds of taxes paid by the business and submit a report that covers the following topics:
        - What is the purpose of each tax?
        - How is each computed?
        - How is each collected?
        - Where does the money go?
    b. Identify at least four kinds of taxes (other than income taxes) you might expect to pay as a citizen. Answer the same questions suggested in (a) above and add two more:
        - Do you understand and agree with each tax?
        - What alternatives might you suggest?

4. List three work-related regulations or codes that apply to your community site and discuss the following questions with your resource person and school staff:
   - Who enforces these regulations?
   - What is their purpose?
   - Does your resource person feel the codes are serving their purpose?
   - What are the good and bad points of the codes as you see them?
   - How do these codes affect you as a citizen?
   - How can ineffective codes be changed?

5. Practicing citizenship
   a. Provide a working definition of citizenship.
   b. Define the term "lobby."
   c. List five ways citizens can participate in the decision-making process at the city, county, regional, state, or national level.
   d. Explain why such participation is essential in a democracy.
   e. Select one activity from each of the following groups:

   Group A
   (1) Attend a meeting of your local city council.
   (2) Attend a meeting of your local school board.
   (3) Attend a meeting of another governing body approved by the staff.

   Group B
   Select an issue or candidate and at the above meeting either:
   (1) Speak on behalf of the issue or candidate.
   (2) Speak in opposition to the issue or candidate.
   (3) Write a statement on behalf of the issue or candidate.
   (4) Write a statement in opposition to the issue or candidate.

   Group C
   (1) Attend and/or participate in a lobbying activity.
   (2) Join and participate in a citizen action group.
   (3) Help conduct a political poll.
   (4) Volunteer some time to a local public interest or community service group.
   (5) Locate and meet a precinct leader and become involved in a precinct activity.
   (6) Write a letter to the editor and get it published.

Possible Products: Reports, written statements, taped interviews, photographic displays, published letter, participation in community activities, organization charts

The Middle School Years

The Citizenship Education Experiences Project of the Rochester (Minnesota) Public Schools contains activities designed to meet the special developmental needs of students between the ages of nine and thirteen. Sample activities from one unit — "Participating in Local Government: A Sixth-Grade Unit" — illustrate these efforts. These activities can be readily adapted for use at other grade levels. They provide strategies for:

- Identifying current local issues and decisions.
- Exploring decisions, services, and attitudes associated with local government.
- Involving local government officials as sources of information.
- Using information and skills in becoming a part of local government decision-making.

All of these activities provide opportunities to use experiences from the students' lives.

CITIZENSHIP GROUNDED IN COMMUNITY

GETTING YOU STARTED

Have things gone well today? Do you have that good feeling that you get when you know you are doing your math right? Are you looking forward to doing something special after school?

Now, let's look a little more closely at your day — what you've done already — what you will do. Just complete the chart on this page. It shouldn't be hard or boring — it's about a very interesting person — YOU!

	ACTION		DECIDER
1.	When did you get up this morning?	1.	Who decided that it was time for you to get up?
2.	What are you wearing today?	2.	Who decided what you were going to wear today?
3.	What time did school start?	3.	Who decides when school will start?
4.	When did you have social studies?	4.	Who decided when you would do your fun social studies?
5.	What movie would you like to see?	5.	Who decides what movies you see?
6.	When will you go to bed tonight?	6.	Who decides when you will go to bed?

After completing these questions individually, students should focus on the frequency with which they listed themselves as the decider, how many of the deciders they argue with when they don't like the decision, and which decisions they accept with little or no protest.

After this consideration of personal actions and the decisions which determine them, students can expand their focus to include impersonal rules and laws. In addition to examining who makes the rules, students can consider reasons for rules and the roles of those who enforce them. Students working in pairs can list two classroom rules, two school rules, and two city ordinances. For each rule and ordinance, they should discover why it exists, who made it, and who enforces it.

When students have shared the information they have gathered, they should consider which rules should be changed and how they could get them changed. This discussion will introduce the students to the idea that rules and laws are not static, but can be modified or nullified through appropriate action. Students also begin to see that voting is only one way to influence decisions.

The following assignment is intended to help students to understand current issues being considered by local government — issues of personal significance to the students' families and in which students can become involved.

ZEROING IN ON LOCAL GOVERNMENTS

Local governments affect our daily lives in hundreds of ways — ways we never even think about.
- What would happen if we didn't have clear, fresh water coming into our homes and schools?
- Suppose that your street or road was never plowed in winter?
- If someone breaks into your home, who do you go to for help?
- How would you find a job if you couldn't get an education?

Well, perhaps you've gotten the idea — *local governments are a very important part of our lives.*

ASSIGNMENT

Later in this unit you will be dealing with problems and issues being considered by local governments. The following assignment is to get you ready for the work you will be doing in future lessons.

In the next three days you should bring to school at least one newspaper article or written report based on a television or radio broadcast. Your article or report must be about a problem or issue being considered by local government. And you must be able to talk about it.

_____ Check here when you have brought an article or report to school.

_____ Check here when you have discussed a local issue or problem with your classmates.

Younger students will probably have to be shown where problems being considered by local government are likely to be found in the newspaper — i.e., the editorial page, local news section, letters to the editor. Upper elementary students often have difficulty distinguishing between national, state, and local issues. Depending on the size of the community and other local characteristics, the elementary teacher may wish to group school district, city, and county government all under the heading of "local government," while the high school teacher can draw finer distinctions. In either case — especially for the elementary student—it is not the structure of government that is at issue here, but rather government as local people acting together to make decisions.

Exploring Local Decisions, Services, and Attitudes

Having examined decisions and rules — who makes them, why they are made, and how they might be changed — the students can consider:
- the kinds of *decisions* that local governments make that affect their lives.
- the *services* that local governments provide to their families.
- public *attitudes* about those decisions and services.

A homework assignment such as the following can help students to focus on these topics.

LOCAL GOVERNMENT — WHO NEEDS IT?

Most people — students and adults alike — know very little about their own local government. "Who cares?" you might say. "Government doesn't affect me anyway." Actually, local government is making decisions and providing services that affect you and your family every day.

DECISIONS MADE FOR YOU

_____ What school you will attend.	_____ Rules and codes that tell you what you can build on your property and how it must be built.
_____ What things you will be taught in school (classes, values, morals).	_____ For what purposes can you use your property—residential, commercial, other.
_____ The rules you must follow while in school.	
_____ The value of your property and how much tax you must pay on it.	_____ What you will pay for public utilities (electricity and water)
_____ Whether or not you will be bused to school.	_____ Whether or not you can water your lawn.
_____ How the money you pay for taxes will be spent.	_____ Rules and licenses for your pets.
_____ Rules and regulations that you must follow in your community.	

1. Can you think of any other decisions made by local governments that might affect you?
2. Place an "X" by any of the decisions in the chart (or others you thought of) that you feel should not be made by your local government. Who do you think would decide these things?
3. Do you think your local government is making wise decisions for you? Explain why or why not.
4. If you feel that local government is not making a wise decision, what might you do about it?
5. Place an "X" by any of the services listed below that would be difficult for your family to provide for itself.

SERVICES USUALLY PROVIDED BY LOCAL GOVERNMENT

_____ Public education	_____ Water
_____ Police protection	_____ Electricity
_____ Fire department	_____ Landfill for refuse
_____ Public library	_____ Civic auditorium
_____ Sanitation system	_____ Paved streets and roads
_____ Parks	_____ Vocational and technical institute
_____ Golf courses	_____ Airport
_____ Recreation center for public activities	_____ Community planning for future development
_____ Animal control and dog pound	_____ Building and housing inspection
_____ Local, state, and federal elections	

6. What services — if any — would you like government to add to make life better for your family?
7. Do you have any criticisms of the services provided by your local government? Do you feel that any service is unnecessary? Do you feel that any service ought to be provided in another way?

This kind of activity can be completed with the help of family members, thus involving parents in the education of their children. However, problems can arise if home surveys are used too often or if parents are less than candid concerning their feelings about local government. Certainly, it would be unfortunate if parents applauded the efficiency of local government and the wisdom of elected officials while they helped their child with the assignment for school, and then complained during dinner about government waste and corruption. However, it would be even worse if parent and child saw the assignment as an opportunity to express honest concern, and then the child reported to a classroom where free and open discussion of those issues was not allowed. Obviously, classroom discussion of attitudes toward government should provide an opportunity to express dissatisfaction with local government, as well as satisfaction with decisions or services. In either case, the focus should be on the reasons for the opinions and on proposals for solving or exploring problems.

Local Officials as Sources

Bringing local officials into the classroom as guest speakers, or having pairs of students interview them and report back to the class, is another way of obtaining current information about local government. Establishing a speaker's bureau designed to serve an entire school district requires considerable work, including active help of government officials, parents, students, teachers, and administrators. However, once such a bureau is established, individual teachers can easily draw on this valuable resource.

Contact with local government officials can help students to identify and clarify local issues in which they might become involved. Strategies like those described earlier in this chapter can stimulate ideas about possible guest speakers. Names and phone numbers of city, school district, and county officials can be found in the telephone book or in directories published by each of these organizations.

The greatest obstacle to obtaining guest speakers is making the first phone call. Overcoming this reluctance can be well worth the effort, inasmuch as face-to-face contact with those involved in local government can greatly influence students' civic participation. Skills in the areas of data gathering and critical thinking can also be enhanced as students prepare questions and analyze the responses of speakers.

Leaders in local government — especially elected officials — are almost always willing to speak to students. It is advisable for teachers to give them some guidelines in advance, however. Speakers might be asked to address such questions as the following:
• What decisions do you and your department make that affect students and their families?

- What services do you provide?
- How do you gauge citizens' feelings about particular issues?
- What do you like most and least about your job?

Questions generated by students could also be included.

Teachers may find it useful to have each student submit a written question prior to the guest speaker's visit. Previous experiences using the media and family members as sources of information will help the students in developing their questions. The teacher can use these questions to stimulate interest and can assist students in refining their questions if necessary. Finally, the size of the group the guest speaker addresses should be limited to one class. Although it may be tempting to invite the classroom next door to hear the mayor or some other important official, the increased size of the group hinders the interaction between the speaker and students which is the real value of this type of activity.

Involving Students in Local Government Decisions

One way to demonstrate to students that they are citizens *now* — not merely being prepared for citizenship rights and responsibilities at some later date — is to involve them directly in decisions of local government. Students need to see that their participation can make a difference. After reviewing the various local issues which they have identified through the media and information gained from parents and guest speakers, students can undertake an assignment such as the following.

DON'T JUST SIT THERE—DO SOMETHING!

You have seen several examples of how citizens can affect the decisions made by local government. You can and should also be involved as a responsible citizen. Don't just sit there — follow the steps below and get involved!

Step 1: Identify the Issue or Problem
Listen to the radio, watch the local news on television, or read the newspaper to discover issues currently being discussed in your community. Choose an issue you find interesting and describe it.

Step 2: Identify the Alternatives
There are always a number of solutions to any problem. Identify alternative solutions to the issue you described above.

Congratulations! You have accomplished the first step to being a responsible citizen. You are aware of a problem in your community and know possible solutions to it. Don't stop now. Go on to Step 3.

Step 3: Identify the Consequences
Before you can make a *responsible* decision about this problem, you must consider more than just the possible solutions. Each solution may have different consequences for yourself and other people in your community. For each solution you listed in Step 2, write the possible consequences (outcomes).

Step 4: Making a Decision
You are now ready to make a responsible decision. Review the alternatives and the possible consequences. Based on your own beliefs, decide which solution provides the best outcome. Write a paragraph explaining your solution and why you think it is the best one.

You have now identified a local issue, studied possible solutions and consequences, and reached a responsible decision. Hang in there — only one step left!

Step 5: Acting on Your Decision
Making a decision is great, but not really enough. A responsible citizen also *acts* on his or her decision. Listed below are some ways in which you can act to influence the outcome on this issue. Choose at least one and get involved.

- Write a letter to the editor of your local paper or a guest column explaining why people should support your solution to the issue.

- Write a letter to a government official involved in this issue (mayor, city council member, county board member, school board member, etc.).

- Attend a meeting being held on this issue.

- Discuss this issue with a parent or other adults to try to convince them to accept your views.

- Volunteer to help a citizens group promote its views on this issue.

- Conduct a poll to find out where citizens stand on this issue.

- Make a poster that promotes your point of view on this issue.

- Other (describe). _____

Teachers may need to explain the decision-making process involved in this assignment before students begin work on a local issue. They should also help students define alternatives and consequences. Examining school or personal problems will familiarize students with this process and prepare them for dealing with more complex issues of local government.

Student Action

The strategies described above are designed to help students identify and become involved in local issues. The following examples of actual projects might be shared with students to give them confidence to carry citizenship beyond the classroom. Although all of these projects were carried out by sixth graders, similar projects might be undertaken by older students. These projects are a small sample of the work done by about 900 students in some 20 elementary schools. All projects have at least three things in common. First, they were introduced by the strategies described above. Second, the issue or problem was selected by the students, with the teacher acting as facilitator. Third, the projects were taken on by students working in small groups, with about seven projects conducted in each classroom.

PARK SAFETY

After three of their classmates were attacked or threatened in a city park near school, a group of sixth graders contacted local police, requesting a foot patrol for the park. Although they were unsuccessful in getting an officer assigned to the park, the students did take positive action. They contacted residents whose homes overlooked the park, informed them of the problems, and requested that they call police if they observed any suspicious activity. The students also made posters informing fellow students of the dangers of walking alone in the park.

RIGHTS OF THE HANDICAPPED

Several students noticed that cars without handicap stickers were parked in spaces designated for the handicapped at a local grocery store. These students made posters to place on the door of the grocery store, reminding customers of the purpose of the specially designated parking spaces. They also spent some of their own time at the entrance of the grocery store and politely asked violators to move their cars.

STUDENT SURVEYS

Students and other members of the community were polled on a wide range of topics, including vandalism, hunting violations, downtown development, proposed construction of a discount store, snow removal, and the growing population of geese at a local lake. Survey results were publicized in a variety of ways. Some students presented their results, complete with graphs and charts, at city council meetings. Others shared the information with appropriate department heads in city government. Indeed, several surveys were conducted at the request of city officials who wanted a better understanding of where their constituents stood on a particular issue. Several students shared their results with the community. Some students took a public stand on local issues by writing letters to the editor or drawing political cartoons for publication in the local newspaper.

SCHOOL ISSUES

Many students selected school district decisions as the focus of their projects. One group set out to examine the reasons for funding cuts in the school lunch program and worked to gain a voice in planning the menus. Earlier, a study of student preferences had resulted in some changes in the menu. Another group of students explored policies of the school district relating to Christmas songs and decorations in classrooms. A large number of sixth graders became involved in the decision-making process concerning a change in the boundary lines for attendance at the junior high schools. Students conducted polls, wrote letters to school administrators, and attended school board meetings.

PARK AND RECREATION BOARD DECISIONS

Because of cutbacks affecting extracurricular activities offered by the school district, students increasingly rely upon programs offered by the Park and Recreation Board—a department of the city government. Students became involved in monitoring board meetings at which decisions affecting activities were made. Students also conducted surveys of young people, recommending possible improvements in activities offered by the Park and Recreation Board.

All student projects were not as successful as those described above. Some students felt that they were not taken seriously by adult members of the community. Others reported to the class that the public meetings they attended were long and dull. Some were unable to complete their work because of personality conflicts with classmates working on the same project. Problems like these provide some excellent teaching opportunities, such as the chance to review strategies for working cooperatively in small groups. Students' complaints about "not being taken seriously" or "dull meetings" reflect some of the realities of community life and need to be dealt with honestly and openly in the classroom.

Concluding Thoughts

Participatory citizenship requires personal engagement in communities familiar to the student—the classroom community, the school community, and the neighborhood community, among others. The following ten questions are to guide teachers in selecting and developing citizenship experiences.

1. Does the citizenship experience relate to the student as someone who is a citizen *now* — not merely as someone being prepared for citizenship rights and responsibilities at some later date? (Conrad and Hedin, 1977).

2. Does the citizenship experience contribute to the students' self-confidence? "... the belief in one's competence is a key political attitude. The self-confident citizen appears to be the democratic citizen. Not only does he think he can participate, he thinks that others ought to participate as well. Furthermore, he does not merely think he can take a part in politics: he is likely to be more active. And, perhaps more significant, the self-confident citizen is also likely to be the more satisfied and loyal citizen" (Almond and Verba, 1965, pp. 206–207).

3. Does the citizenship experience avoid mere indoctrination? Indoctrination not only fails to provide students with the skills required to deal with current issues, but is also incompatible with the principles of a free society (Osborn et al., 1979).

4. Is the citizenship experience available to all students—not merely to the academically able, the middle class, or a racially distinct group? (Osborn et al., 1979.)

5. Does the citizenship experience develop a body of knowledge in a functional context? For example, students can learn about the structure of the city council while exploring how the council makes decisions, how those decisions affect students, and how students can influence those decisions.

6. Does the citizenship experience facilitate free and open discussion of controversial issues? Although curriculum materials alone cannot create an open classroom climate, they may encourage it. Open classroom climate tends to promote a sense of trust and competence (Ehman, 1980).

7. Does the citizenship experience stimulate and guide reflection by the learners? Although reflective activities may take many forms, the emphasis should be on self-analysis by the students (Remy, n.d.).

8. Is the citizenship experience personally meaningful to the students? It should draw upon phenomena students encounter in their daily lives as

citizens within local institutions. At the same time, it should include activities or questions which provide practice in generalizing from familiar personal experiences to situations outside the students' immediate experience (Remy, n.d.).

9. Does the citizenship experience reinforce earlier activities without boring repetition? Cognitive, emotional, and physical attributes of the student's age must be taken into account. Also, connections between knowledge and skills developed in other subject areas and earlier citizenship experiences should be made wherever possible (Remy, n.d.).

10. Does the citizenship experience include active learning by students? For example, students should not only read about making decisions, but also practice making them. Active learning may be accomplished through experiences such as real events and simulations (Remy, n.d.).

Bibliography

Almond, G. A., and Verba, S. *The Civic Culture.* Boston: Little, Brown and Company, 1965.

Bayles, E. E. "Education for Democracy." *Kansas Studies in Education,* 8:11, No. 2, May 1958. Lawrence, KS: School of Education, University of Kansas.

Conrad, D., and Hedin, D. "Citizenship Education through Participation," in *Education for Responsible Citizenship: The Report of the National Task Force on Citizenship Education,* New York: McGraw-Hill Book Company, 1977.

Dawson, R. E., Prewitt, K. D., and Dawson, K. S. *Political Socialization.* Second Edition, Boston: Little Brown, 1977.

Ehman, L. H. "American School in the Political Socialization Process." *Review of Educational Research,* Spring 1980, 110–113.

Gillespie, J., and Lazarus, S. *Comparing Political Experiences Political Issues Skills Kit.* Social Studies Curriculum Development Center, Bloomington, IN.

National Assessment of Educational Progress, *Changes in Political Knowledge and Attitudes, 1969–1976.* Denver, CO, 1978.

Newmann, F. M. *Education for Citizen Action—Challenge for Secondary Curriculum.* Berkeley: McCutchan Publishing Corporation, 1975.

Newmann, F. M., Bertocci, T. A., and Landsness, R. M. *Skills in Citizen Action: An English-Social Studies Program for Secondary Schools.* Madison, WI: Citizen Participation Curriculum Project, 1977.

McClure, L., Cook, S. C., and Thompson, V. *Experience-Based Learning: How To Make the Community Your Classroom.* Portland, OR: Northwest Regional Educational Laboratory, 1977.

Naisbitt, J. *Megatrends: Ten New Directions Transforming Our Lives.* New York: Warner Books, 1982.

Osborn, R., et al., "Revision of the NCSS Social Studies Curriculum Guidelines." *Social Education,* April 1979.

Remy, R. C. *Handbook of Basic Citizenship Competencies.* Alexandria, VA: Association for Supervision and Curriculum Development, n.d.

Yankelovich, D. *New Rules: Searching for Self-Fulfillment in a World Turned Upside Down.* New York: Random House, 1981.

CHAPTER VII / DIANE HEDIN

Developing Values Through Community Service

At the end of a presentation by several teenagers about their volunteer work in social agencies, a member of the audience hostilely interrogates the panelists: "That's fine for kids like you, but what would you suggest I do? I work with delinquents — tough, violent guys who wouldn't be caught dead helping anybody." Colin, 17, unkempt, with long, stringy hair and a perpetually sullen expression, responds: "Mister, I've got to straighten you out. I've been in so many homes and schools, whatever you call them, for dealing drugs, burglary — you name it. What you guys do doesn't help. It didn't help me, but they let me out anyway. Then I started going to this nursing home through this class in school and helping out there. I just talk to those old people, play the piano, shoot a little pool with some of the old guys, take them for walks. And you know what — they like me. The old ladies say I'm just like their grandsons. This is the first time I've ever done anything for anybody, and it's helped me more than 10,000 group meetings."

At the beginning of the school year, Bob held extreme racist attitudes about blacks. When he first went to the day-care center in an inner-city community, he sat stiffly and tossed a ball back and forth with the little boys. He cringed when the children came too near. "You let those black things touch you?" he asked one girl who played easily with the children. When she looked surprised, he added gruffly, "When you go to eat, just be sure to wash your hands." This same young man, a few months later, is met at the door by a small black child who grins widely at the sight of him. He swings the child into the air and laughs at his upside-down expression. Later, he discusses the child's latest "clever" comments with his friends, expressing genuine pride in "his" little kid.

The 1980's — and the preceding decades — have witnessed a great deal of public concern about the level of personal, moral, and social responsibility exhibited by adolescents. Charges that adolescents are becoming increasingly private, hedonistic, narcissistic, and aimless have become commonplace. One observer (Senesh, 1980) has described our youth as a "cut-flower" generation — a generation which has lost its community roots. The most visible participation by youth in civic affairs — its turnout at the polls — has been abysmal. Less than 20 percent of the 18- to 21-year-olds even bothered to vote in the 1980 presidential election.

Youth's pessimism and cynicism about American society has shown a persistent upward trend. In the 1980 Monitoring the Future Study, 65 percent of 17,000 high school seniors in 130 high schools across the nation said that they thought things in their community and society would be "worse or much worse" in five years. Pessimism about the future of the country jumped 20 percentage points from 1978 to 1980.

By contrast, adolescents remain cheerfully optimistic about their personal futures. When asked, "How do you think things in your own life will go in the next 5 years?" 84 percent said "better or much better," while only 3 percent said "worse." These data might indicate that adolescents feel powerless to affect events in the outside world — the local, national, and international communities — while at the same time believing that they can take charge of their personal lives. Further evidence for this hypothesis is found in the Monitoring the Future Study. High school seniors ranked having a good marriage and family life as their most important goal as adults, and taking leadership in their community as their least important goal (Bachman, Johnston, and O'Malley, 1975, 1980). A similar finding comes from the studies by the National Center for Educational Statistics, which indicate a sharp decline in the percentage of high school seniors concerned about "working to correct social and economic inequalities." In 1972, 27 percent of students surveyed thought it was important or very important; by 1980, that percentage had declined to 13 percent (U.S. Department of Education, 1981).

Counteracting feelings of powerlessness, alienation, and narcissism among the young requires more immediate experiences than those offered by the typical lecture and recitation structure of many social studies classrooms. Even the most widely used approaches to moral and values education — discussion of hypothetical moral dilemmas or classroom activities in values clarification — appear to have mixed success in leading adolescents to act in more socially responsible ways. Lawrence Kohlberg, the leading theoretician in the moral education movement, has himself called for more active approaches to the development and stimulation of moral judgment in adolescents (1979). Kohlberg has become involved in designing "just communities," where students are responsible for governance of their classroom and school as the context for moral discussion, values education, and responsible action.

Another promising approach to stimulating moral growth has been to involve adolescents in the life of their local community in new roles such as community service providers, researchers, and social and political activists. This chapter will describe some of this work and its rationale. But before we turn to this discussion, it is important to clarify what is meant by moral development.

Moral Development

Knowledge about value or moral development is based upon cognitive developmental theory as articulated by Piaget, Kohlberg, Gilligan, and Selman, whose research indicates that people develop in a series of qualitatively distinct stages. They assume that all humans ponder questions such as the meaning of human experience, what is right and wrong, and under what conditions one human being will help another. The form those questions take and the ways in which the answers are determined are distinctively different depending upon the individual's stage of development. Further, a developmental approach assumes that children and adolescents are capable of moving toward altruistic and just perspectives on relationships among human beings.

Sprinthall and Collins (1983) note that approximately 50 percent of adolescents start junior high school with a highly individualistic perspective. They follow rules only when it is it their immediate interest, and the basic motive is to satisfy their own needs. By age 15, many adolescents are no longer exclusively concerned with materialistic rewards, but instead are concerned with living up to what is expected by the people closest to them, such as family and friends. Now the basic motives are to be accepted and to conform to the values of the group. Value choices are increasingly other-directed.

Most adolescents remain at this level throughout their high school years, strongly subject to the influence of others. While we usually think of the peer group as determining adolescents' values, teenagers are equally susceptible to certain charismatic adults.

A minority of adolescents — less than 20 percent — comes to view justice as fulfilling personal duties and upholding the law. At this level of moral reasoning, a person tends to apply a standard of law and order rigidly, regardless of circumstances. Kohlberg has found almost no high school students with a clear understanding of the universality of democratic principles such as individual freedom, justice for all, due process of law, free speech, majority will, minority rights, and equality before the law (Colby, Kohlberg, and Gibbs, 1979).

These findings indicate that adolescents do not leave secondary school with the ability needed to live as active, informed citizens in a democratic society. There is evidence that students are capable of higher-level reasoning during high school, yet most do not use that model. Research indicates that human character, to use an old-fashioned term, can be stimulated by certain kinds of educational experiences. The great strides in research in developmental psychology in the last decade have made it possible to formulate in rather specific terms what stimulates movement to the next higher stage of moral and value development. These advances, in turn, allow us to determine appropriate educational interventions for helping adolescents, at various stages of development, to move toward higher levels of maturity.

While a great deal of attention has been devoted to clarifying and developing valuing processes, there needs to be greater concern with moral action. The way in which people decide what they ought to do, what is right and wrong, and what their obligations and rights are is critical to their moral philosophy. But thinking about moral issues is not enough. The moral issues of our community, country, and world cry out for people who have moral courage to move from analysis to action.

Factors Leading to Moral Growth

What kinds of experiences stimulate moral development, both in thought and in action? Some examples follow:

1. *Confronting alternative perspectives.* To perceive or experience different points of view allows adolescents to move out of a self-centered view of the world until they can actually see themselves from an external perspective. The opportunity to interact with persons different from themselves brings adolescents into contact with moral positions that conflict with their own. Experiences in the wider community which expose students to people who are different in age, social class, occupation, race, and ethnic background are particularly helpful in that they broaden opportunities for role-taking beyond the usual cast of characters in junior and senior high school — the students' peers and their teachers.

2. *Experiencing challenges.* It is necessary for a person to confront situations and decisions which challenge his or her value system in order for growth to occur. These challenges produce anxiety which leads to the development of new ways of thinking in order to respond to these crises. Teachers can promote moral growth by providing students with provocative, challenging problems which force them to examine their current beliefs. While it is possible to create such conflicts through reading, role-playing, and films, using the wider community expands such opportunities significantly.

3. *Matching experiences to the student's stage of moral and social development.* For optimal moral growth, students should be engaged at their own level of reasoning in experiences which will challenge them to exercise their skills in more sophisticated ways. They must not be overwhelmed with demands beyond their current level. In general, appropriate learning activities for adolescents strike a balance between actual experience and careful reflective examination of the meaning of that experience.

Based on research in developmental education, some generalizations can be made about the kinds of educational experiences which are most appropriate to adolescents' levels of moral reasoning:

- Peer counseling seems to be a powerful device to help students see things from another perspective.
- The study of law and government combined with involvement in community service and social or political action are appropriate experiences for adolescents.
- Role-taking experiences where students must understand people different from themselves are appropriate experiences. Examples include interviewing people of different ages and cross-age teaching with students very different from themselves.
- Experiences in making rules and governing schools and school organizations democratically, as well as attempts to influence public policy and intern-

ships in government and regulatory agencies, seem to be effective ways to help students move to higher levels of reasoning (Hedin, 1979).

4. *Action opportunities.* The opportunity to act provides the most important test of moral reasoning. Does the young person have the courage to act on his or her moral convictions? As Dewey has argued, the ultimate test of the value of an educational program is its "use and application in carrying out and improving the common life for all" (Dewey, 1934, 1964). Though the correspondence of judgment and action is never simple, there is evidence that better judgment may lead to more consistent social behavior (Selman, 1976).

Community Service Programs

Serving as volunteers in nursing homes, day-care centers, elementary schools, hospitals, counseling centers, and institutions for mentally, physically, or emotionally handicapped people can provide adolescents with opportunities for combining significant and responsible work in social agencies with ongoing reflection about that field experience. There are several exemplary social studies courses around the country which require teenagers to take on the ethical responsibilities of helping and being responsive to other human beings. These class periods are typically two hours in length, and students spend at least three-fourths of their time in their field assignments and remainder in the classroom examining that experience. The two-hour block of time is necessary for students to travel to and from their field sites and have sufficient time to make a worthwhile contribution there.

What do students actually do in their field assignments? It is essential that students' field experiences involve working directly with the people served by the agency rather than doing clerical or custodial duties. If community service is to encourage moral growth, then it is necessary for students to learn the complex skills involved in actual interpersonal relationships. A study of 33 experiential education programs in high schools across the country indicated that certain characteristics of the field experience had a strong impact on student growth. The best predictors of personal and social growth were opportunities for autonomy — e.g., situations in which students felt free to put their own ideas into action — and collegial relationships with and guidance by adults in positions of authority at the field site (Conrad and Hedin, 1981).

The actual tasks which students perform vary widely. A tutor or teacher for elementary students may lead a reading group of slow learners, provide individual help to pupils, teach a mini-course in an area of personal interest such as bike repair or prehistoric animals, or serve as a discussion leader on topics such as drug or value education. A volunteer in a nursing home may provide companionship, write letters for residents, help feed those who need assistance, organize a recreation program, or conduct daily physical exercises. A peer counselor may be assigned to a lonely junior high student who needs help in making friends, work in a teenage health clinic providing information about birth control and sexuality, or staff a drop-in center for pre-delinquent youth. With funding for human services declining, many social agencies would particularly welcome the energy and skills of adolescents. Many community service programs which have been in existence for a few years report having more requests for student volunteers than they are able to meet.

There are several approaches to assigning students to field sites. In some cases, a community involvement fair is held at the beginning of the semester. Representatives of community agencies set up booths and explain the needs and function of their agency and the kind of help students can provide. The student can arrange, on the spot, a mutually satisfying contract with the agency representatives. In other programs, the class visits a series of potential field sites to take a look firsthand at the organization. This has the side benefit of enlarging the student's knowledge about community services and organizations, even if the student does not actually volunteer at that site. If neither site visits nor a fair can be arranged, having community agency representatives come to class to explain their programs and volunteer needs would be effective.

Matching Students to Placements

As described earlier, maximum growth results if students participate in experiences that are appropriately matched to their current level of development. Perry (1968) has suggested that students need to be challenged and supported. While challenge is necessary to induce adolescents to surpass their current ways of processing experiences, it should not be excessive, or the individual may retreat or resist further development.

How can an appropriate "mismatch" be built into the experiences of each student in a community service course and inappropriate ones be avoided? First, individual students often have good ideas of the kind of volunteer tasks which are suitable for them. Adolescents usually know what level of challenge and responsibility they can handle. In addition, research using the work of such developmental theorists as Kohlberg and Loevinger provides some guidelines for matching and sequencing educational experiences. A summary of this work is contained in Table 1, which includes the degree of structure (amount of supervision, approaches to reflection, complexity of tasks) and the types of classroom and field-work activities (cross-age teaching, public policy research) which will produce growth. Brief descriptions of the developmental stages are included to summarize the ways in which adolescents typically think about moral issues at each level. Also included are the corresponding descriptions of Loevinger's stages of ego development, which are useful in identifying the types of interpersonal and cognitive styles used by teenagers. Combining the characteristics of both moral and ego development may help teachers to determine at what level their students typically function.

TABLE 1 EDUCATIONAL EXPERIENCES FOR ADOLESCENTS CATEGORIZED BY DEVELOPMENTAL STATUS

Moral Judgment (Kohlberg)	Ego Development (Loevinger)	Educational Experience
Stage 2 — naively egocentric orientation. Right action is what is instrumentally satisfying to one's needs — i.e., "You scratch my back, I'll scratch yours."	Impulsive — 1–2. Self-protective, exploitive, dependent, short attention span, does not follow through, blames others, wary, concrete and stereotyped thinking.	Structure: Close supervision in field experience. Simple, clear tasks. Grade based on quantity of work and fulfilling a contract. Gradual increments of responsibility and initiative from modest levels. Journal writing, responding to specific questions. Work in teams to develop loyalty and responsibility to others. Types of experiences: Experiences which will elicit empathy or caring, involving persons likely to show appreciation, such as children, senior citizens, or handicapped persons. Cross-age teaching from highly structured curriculum guides. Volunteer work in nursing home or day-care center with specific, clearly defined duties. Discussion of moral dilemmas through role-playing original dilemmas or those encountered in field experience. Peer counseling.
Stage 3 — good-boy/good-girl orientation to approval and to pleasing and helping others. Conformity to stereotypical images of majority or "natural" behavior.	Conformist — 1–3 and 3/4. Conformity to external rules, shame, guilt for breaking rules, need to belong, helpfulness, superficial niceness. Thinking is conceptually simplistic; ideas are clichés.	Structure: Moderately complex tasks. Willing to perform tasks without constant supervision, but seeks approval and recognition from supervisor. Grade based on quantity and quality of work. Team or group work to consolidate this stage; individual work to stimulate movement to next higher stage. Journal writing, responding to a choice of questions related to multiple explanations, causes and the conflict between pleasing others and upholding rules.

DEVELOPING VALUES

Stage 4 — orientation to authority and maintaining social order. Concerned with "doing duty," showing respect for authority, and maintaining the established social order for its own sake. Regard for earned expectations of others.	Conscientious — 1–4, 4/5, and 1–5. Self-evaluated standards, self-criticism, long-term goals, intensive, responsible. Conceptual complexity.	*Types of experiences:* To consolidate stage — caring experiences; work in social and human service agencies. Peer counseling and consultation. Cross-age teaching, with freedom to select activities, methods, materials from curriculum guides. Activities which require development of personal relationships with others. To stimulate higher levels of development — volunteer work related to public affairs, e.g. voter registration or lobbying efforts related to earlier volunteer experience in social service. Participation in just school or democratic classroom, or study of ethics. Peer conseling about sensitive, controversial issues, such as sexual activity or drug use. *Structure:* Abstract, complex tasks. High level of responsibility and initiative. Carry out responsibilities in absence of strong adult supervision and support. Grade based on student's as well as instructor's judgment. Collegial relationships with adults. *Types of experiences:* Research projects. Internships in government, corrections, law, regulatory agencies. Attempts to influence public policy. Peer counseling about sensitive, controversial issues, such as rape and birth control. Cross-age teaching — moral dilemmas, controversial issues where students have freedom to design their own curriculum. Systematic experiences in rule-making and democratic governance of schools.

One does not necessarily need to test the student's level of moral judgment in order to use this matching system. Assessments of developmental status obtained through interviewing and observing students have proven to be quite adequate. Moreover, as stated earlier, adolescents often do "know themselves" and can supply support for the teacher's hunches.

The Role of Field Supervisors

Successful community service programs depend on capable supervisors of students at the site. The primary task of the field supervisor is that any supervisor — to orient the "worker" to the responsibilities and tasks of the job, to structure the tasks so that they are commensurate to the worker's skills and abilities, to provide prompt and clear indications of successes and mistakes, to suggest improvement, and to evaluate the worker's overall performance. In addition, supervisors of adolescents in community service programs are most effective when they possess another set of qualities — they genuinely like and have a reasonably good understanding of teenagers; they view themselves as "educators," and not merely employers; and they are willing to treat teenagers as colleagues, rather than as "kids" or "students."

This final point about the importance of a personal, collegial relationship between supervisor and teenager has several dimensions. First, experience has shown that those supervisors who report having close personal relationships with their teenage volunteers are most likely to rate the program highly. The same finding applies to the teenage volunteers — that is, students are more likely to describe their volunteer experience as excellent if they have enjoyed a close relationship with their supervisor. Moreover, the effective supervisor often serves as an important adult model for the young person — someone to be emulated in terms of career choice and personal qualities. In a follow-up study of a community internship program in Pennsylvania, more than 40 percent of the students surveyed reported having chosen a career path because of their positive experience in the high school internship, and often because they admired their field supervisor.

Finally, the supervisor who is well informed about the purposes and curriculum of the school's community service program will be most capable of providing appropriate training and supervision for the students. This seems like an obvious point. However, a current study of eight community service programs across the nation reveals that almost no supervisor had any knowledge of what the students were learning in the classroom component of the program (Newmann and Rutter, 1983). Merely informing the field supervisor of the content and activities in the seminar could help to make the community service program an integrated, comprehensive experience for the student.

Reflection on the Field Experience

The deliberate blending of experience *and* thought — action *and* reflection — is most likely to promote moral and social development. One study of experiential education referred to earlier (Conrad and Hedin, 1981) found that the presence of an ongoing seminar was crucial to the students' growth. Specifically, students who showed the greatest increases on a measure of empathy and cognitive complexity were those who were given instruction in problem-solving and empathic role-taking in their classroom seminar. Another powerful message about the importance of reflection comes from a study of sixth graders who tutored mentally retarded children (Blum, 1978). Tutors who did not have a supervisory seminar developed increasingly negative attitudes toward the mainstreamed children and employed less effective teaching techniques than they had initially. Tutors who participated in a weekly seminar in which they learned teaching methods are reviewed their experiences showed increased empathy and capacity for role-taking. These findings give solid empirical support to Dewey's notion that experience can have positive or negative educational value, depending upon what the learner and the teacher do with the experience. It is advocated that the learner consciously attend to what is going on by observing, asking questions, comparing and contrasting this experience with others, and forming generalizations and trying to apply these to new experiences. It is this application of intelligence to experience that is called "reflection."

Curricula in Human Development and Helping Skills

Exemplary community service programs in the social studies tend to emphasize three major issues in the classroom seminars — the social psychology of human development, helping skills appropriate to the field placement (counseling, interviewing, teaching, communications skills), and the skills needed to learn from experience. In addition, some attention is typically given to learning about the range of community problems and responses to them, as well as to finding and using governmental and community resources.

The classroom seminar can be productively divided into three separate components: (1) orientation and preparation for the field experience, (2) ongoing reflection and inservice training, and (3) development of a final product to summarize and generalize the learning. A discussion of each component and a suggested set of objectives, as well as sample classroom activities that could accomplish these objectives, follows.

Orientation

The key objectives to be accomplished before the students begin their field work include: getting acquainted; building a sense of community among the students; sensitizing them to the kinds of issues, people, and situations that they may encounter; teaching the basic skills needed in field work, such as listening attentively and responding with empathy; and working on the skills necessary to learn from experience, including the ability to assume multiple perspectives, thereby seeing people in more complex, less stereotyped ways. Space permits us to consider only two of these objectives in detail.

Establishing a sense of belonging is a crucial step toward creating an effective classroom seminar in which young people will freely give help to one another and openly confront dilemmas and challenges in their field work. Such an open, trusting classroom is critical for moral growth. Clearly, a sense of community is not developed through a few opening exercises. The following activity is merely suggestive of a way to begin the process.

PRACTICE INTERVIEWS — DEVELOPING A GROUP PROFILE

This activity is designed to help students assess what they have to offer — both individually and as a group. The benefits of doing this are: (1) it provides practice in being on either side of a personal interview; (2) it provides clearer focus when the exact nature of the program is only generally defined (e.g., to "do something about drug abuse," or "beautify the neighborhood"), on the basis of the unique talents and interests of group members; (3) it defines for each person how his or her own knowledge and skills are magnified and multiplied when combined with those of the others in the group. This is one step in building a group identity: to have individuals begin to think of themselves in terms of their collective power.

Classes should follow these steps:
1. Divide into groups of three. Two members will interview the third about his or her interests, skills, and whatever else may be useful in the program — from why each person is in it, to whether he or she has access to a car. Each interviewer should be taking careful notes. At the end, these will be checked by the person interviewed before being handed in.
   Note: These need to be probing, even "pushy," interviews for them to be productive. People often fear being seen as "braggarts," even more than as incompetents, so it's usually necessary to probe to discover their strengths. It may help to ask about something about personal interests first. It also helps if the teacher models the process beforehand by interviewing one of the students.
2. Have each member of each threesome report to the whole group on what they found out.
3. As interests and skills, etc., are named, write them on a blackboard. When everyone has reported, you will have a profile of what, collectively, the group has to offer the community. Emphasize that to the degree that the class develops as a collective unit, each person has not only his or her own skills to work with, but all of the attributes listed.
4. If the project is fairly well defined at this point, go through the list and brainstorm how each of the attributes listed (from "patience" to "pinball pro") could contribute to the project and to the general welfare and functioning of the group itself.
5. Conclude the exercise by writing a group résumé or an advertisement proclaiming the qualities of the group.

Preparing students for their encounters with people older or younger than themselves, from different social classes or ethnic backgrounds, or with various disabilities might start by sensitizing the students to these differences. For example, a person who will work with handicapped adults might spend a day in a wheelchair to experience the physical and psychological limitations that such a device imposes. Students who will be assigned to work with elementary children might be asked to try to recall what they were like at that age, as a way to reenter the world of the child.

Ongoing Reflective Activities

While the students are in their practicum, the seminar might emphasize any of the following:
- Providing information and academic knowledge about human development.
- Having the students gather firsthand data about community problems and child and adult development.
- Practicing the skills used in their work — e.g., teaching methods, interviewing, verbal and nonverbal communication, and counseling.
- Refining experiential learning skills, such as observing and questioning.
- Enhancing problem-solving skills.
- Helping one another to solve specific problems in their field placements.
- Looking at the relationship between the work of their agency or organization and other social problems.
- Learning about other services and resources beyond those which the class can offer to deal with social problems.

Again, a few examples of how several of these objectives might be pursued are given below:

A technique involving critical incidents can be used effectively to work on several of these objectives simultaneously. Students might be asked to record critical incidents or situations when a person is called upon to act, but when it is not immediately obvious what action should be taken. Being alert for such incidents enhances students' skills of observation and analysis. The "critical" in "critical incident" does not necessarily mean dramatic or conspicuous. In fact, the opposite is usually the case. If a child falls and cuts himself, it is rather easy to decide what to do — easier than if the child seems to be "down on himself," and someone wants to find a way to lift him up. Often what seems "critical" to the thoughtful and involved person is missed completely by the casual observer. Discussing these critical incidents in the classroom can elevate the seminar above the level of mere "show and tell." Instead, it becomes a consultation, in which the resources of the group are combined to solve problems of real concern to individual members.

Such critical incidents offer the opportunity to relate academic knowledge about human development to actual real-life problems. For example, if students are using Maslow's "Hierarchy of Needs" to analyze why some of the children in the elementary class are not attentive to their studies, they might consider the possibility that the children are not eating breakfast (an example of a survival need not being met), or that they feel inferior because of their poor reading skills (an example of a need for esteem not being met). Such discussion can introduce and reinforce the notion that one needs to consider multiple perspectives and explanations of human behavior — a key element in helping adolescents to develop more complex and abstract thinking.

The following critical incident assignment provides a framework for analyzing day-to-day issues using Maslow's theory:

1. Describe an incident or situation that was a critical problem at least in the sense that it was not immediately obvious to you what to do or say.
2. What is the first thing you thought of to do (or say)?
3. List three other actions you might have taken (or things you might have said).
4. Which of these seems best to you now? Why?
5. What do you think is the basic problem in the situation; in other words, why do you think that the situation developed in the first place?

When you are identifying the underlying problem, explain what *need* you think may be causing the person(s) to act or to speak in the way that you have described. You may not have all the information you need, and you may have to "read something into" the situation to make this judgment. But, in doing so, you are at least attempting to see the situation from someone else's point of view.

Observation reports offer another technique for sharpening the student's skills in learning from experience, through careful observation, analysis, and synthesis of these observations with academic knowledge:

1. CASE STUDY
   Assignment: Observe one client or adult co-worker closely over a period of time, taking notes while you are at your placement or immediately afterwards. Look for specific actions, interactions, or comments that seem particularly important. Use concrete details in describing this person's appearance, personality, and behavior in your case study.
2. COMMUNICATION PROBLEMS
   Assignment: Identify and describe one example of a problem that was caused by two people not understanding each other's situation. This communication problem might involve you or it might be between two other people you observe. Be sure to explain the situation well enough that it is clear what caused the problem.
3. SEX-ROLE BEHAVIOR
   Assignment: People learn roles by hearing about them, seeing them, and practicing them. One of the things people must learn is their sex roles (how to be boys and how to be girls). Very early, they learn what they think is appropriate for males to do and for females to do. Often they develop a rather narrow and stereotyped version of what is "appropriate" behavior and then maintain this view throughout life. Sometimes, our social institutions (day-care centers, schools, nursing homes, and businesses) reinforce these narrow views. Your assignment is to (1) observe the behavior of males and females in your field site, and describe a scene in which someone there is learning and/or acting out a stereotyped sex role (e.g., a boy refusing to do "girl stuff"), or where someone is learning and/or acting out a less narrow version of what is appropriate for his or her sex; (2) describe how the place where you work either reinforces, or is trying to broaden, traditional sex role behaviors (through stories, books, activities encouraged, rules, etc.).

Synthesis

To complete the learning cycle and to stimulate maximum cognitive and moral growth, students should develop products which pull together their learning about self, others, and the community. The objectives of this component of the seminar might include: passing on knowledge and expertise to the next group of students, having public documentation of the project, synthesizing the many parts of the experience into a meaningful whole, recording progress toward resolving community problems, and providing suggestions to the instructor for program improvement.

For their final products, students might be asked to:

1. Make a formal presentation on the project to an appropriate audience, such as the city council, school board, agricultural extension agents, service organization, or another class or group of students. The purpose of this activity is to give students the opportunity to tell *some* outside audience what they have achieved.
2. Produce a lasting document on the project: photo essay, videotape, booklet, or slide presentaion. This should show both the achievements and the process in order to help interested persons attempt a similar project.
3. Prepare a "tip sheet" to pass on to future participants some things they have learned. For example, youth working in nursing homes can prepare sheets outlining "Ten Rules for Working with the Elderly."

The reflective activities contained in this article exemplify only a few of the ways in which experiences in the local community can be examined. Many more ideas are contained in a publication entitled *Learning from the Field Experience* by Dan Conrad, which is available from the National Commission on Resources for Youth, 605 Commonwealth Avenue, Boston, Massachusetts 02215, (617) 353-3309.

Conclusion

Studies of community service courses in secondary schools around the country indicate that it is possible to stimulate the moral and social growth of adolescents through their participation in significant and responsible roles in their community. Such new roles include teaching, consulting, facilitating groups, counseling, doing research, interning in government and political organizations, interviewing, and others. The most effective programs contain several common elements and include opportunities for adolescents to do the following:

- Perform tasks which both the students and the community regard as significant and worthwhile;
- Make decisions that have real consequences for others as well as themselves;
- Consider genuine social and moral conflicts;
- Gain new skills and new knowledge to carry out their responsibilities; and
- Take action on behalf of chosen social and moral goals.

While this chapter has focused primarily on the gains for the individual young person from such participation, there are benefits to the local community as well. Adolescents can help to solve local community problems ranging from caring for preschool children to working on consumer fraud. At a time when there are fewer public funds available for all the human services, it becomes all the more important for adolescents to be enlisted in the struggle for a just and equitable society. Those of us who are concerned about *both* the development of individual human beings and the improvement of society as a whole must forcefully assert that neither goal is well served by restricting adolescents to classroom study of community problems. The achievement of a central task of social studies education — helping children and youth think and act sensitively and humanely on the basic moral and social justice questions facing the world of the future — requires the young to take on moral and social responsibilities today.

Bibliography

Bachman, J. G., Johnston, L. D., and O'Malley, P. M. *Monitoring the Future: A Continuing Study of the Lifestyles and Values of Youth.* Ann Arbor: Institute for Social Research, The University of Michigan, 1975, 1980.

Blum, L. A. *A Model of Transition Mainstreaming: A Cross-Cognitive Tutor Program.* Unpublished doctoral dissertation, University of Minnesota, 1978.

Colby, A., Kohlberg, L., and Gibbs, J. "The Measurement of Stages of Moral Judgment." Final Report to the National Institute of Mental Health. Cambridge, MA: Center for Moral Development and Education, 1979.

Conrad, D., and Hedin, D. *Executive Summary, Experiential Education Evaluation Project.* St. Paul: Center for Youth Development and Research, University of Minnesota, 1981.

Dewey, J. "The Need for a Philosophy of Education," in *John Dewey on Education,* (ed.). R. D. Archambault. Chicago: The University of Chicago Press, 1964. (Originally published, 1934).

Hedin, D. P. *Teenage Health Educators: An Action Learning Program to Promote Psychological Development.* Unpublished doctoral dissertation, University of Minnesota, 1979.

Kohlberg, L. "Foreword," in *Promoting Moral Growth,* R. H. Hersh, D. P. Paolitto, and J. Reimer (eds.). New York: Longman, 1979.

Kluckhohn, C., and Murray, H. A. (eds.). *Personality in Nature, Society, and Culture.* New York: Alfred A. Knopf, 1948.

Mosher, R. L. *Adolescent's Development and Education.* Berkeley, CA: McCutchan, 1979.

Newmann, F. M. and Rutter, R. *The Effects of High School Community Service Programs on Students' Social Development.* University of Wisconsin—Madison, Center for Education Research: Final Report to the National Institute of Education, Grant Number NIE-G-81-0009, December, 1983.

Perry, W. G., Jr. *Intellectual and Ethical Development in the College Years.* New York: Holt, Rinehart and Winston, 1968.

Selman, R. "A Developmental Approach to Interpersonal and Moral Awareness," in *Values and Moral Development,* T. Hennesey (ed.). New York: Paulist Press, 1976, 142–166.

Senesh L. "The Community Profile: A Tool to Improve Economic Competence." *Peabody Journal of Education,* April, 1980, 163–166.

Sprinthall, N., and Collins, A. *Adolescent Psychology: A Developmental View.* Reading, MA: Addison Wesley, 1983.

United States Department of Education. *The High School and Beyond.* Washington, DC: National Center for Educational Statistics, 1981.

Index

A
Advisory Committees, 12
Agee, James (photographer), 68
Ah-Gwah-Ching Historical Society, 68
American Field Service, 28
American Political Science Association, 77
Amish, 62
ANTHROS Project, 28
Arizona, 28
Arkansas, 28, 67
Armstrong, Arthur, (American Artist), 59
Apple Computers, 30
Archaeology and artifacts, 13, 41, 53

B
Baltimore, Maryland, 59, 62
Basic Economics Test (Grades 4–6), 39
Beissel, Johann Conrad (Pietist), 62
Bierstadt, Albert (American artist), 58
Boston, Massachusetts, 59
Boston Computer Society, 30

C
Caldwell, Erskine, 68
California, 30
Calverts, the, 59
Calvinist theology, 59
Catalogs, mail order (of the past), 53
Chamber of Commerce (as source), 33, 40
Chelmsford, Massachusetts, 30
Chicago, Illinois, 34
Chicano community, St. Paul, Minnesota, 44, 45, 65
Citizenship education, 2, 8, 82–83
Colonial South, 59
Community resources, 16
Community service (as learning tool), 8–10
Community study, 3–6, 8, 11
Comprehension, student, 3
Copley, John Singleton, (portraitist), 59
Corcoran Gallery of Art, 71
Curricular materials, developing, 6, 7
Curriculum planning, 11

D
Democratic beliefs and practices, 11, 13
DePaul Center for Economic Education, 34
Distrust between community and school, 5
Duluth, Minnesota, 59

E
Economics education, 29
Eicholtz, Jacob, 59

Employment, conflict with schoolwork, 31
Ephrata County, Pennsylvania, 62
Evans, Walker (photographer), 68
Evanston, Illinois, 28

F
Federal Art Project (WPA), 66, 67
Fieldtrips, 6–8, 12, 26–27, 34–37
Florida, 44
Foreign investment, 25–26
Fredericksburg, Texas, 60

G
Gardner, David, 30
Geography, 13, 24, 27, 41
Georgia, 71
German-Americans, New Ulm, Minnesota, 45
German Immigrants in Texas, 60
Gilcrease Museum, Tulsa, Oklahoma, 66
"Graco — A Case Study . . . .", 33
Grand Canyon, 58

H
Hassett, Greg, 30
Herr, Hans (Mennonite), 62
"hierarchy of needs" (Maslow's), 104–105
Hogue, Alexander, (American artist), 66
Hurd, Nathaniel, 59

I
Illinois, 28
Immigrants as guest speakers, 22–23
Indiana, 28
Indiana University, 28
Internships, economic field, 34

J
Jobs, Steve, 30
Johnson, Eastman (American artist), 59
Joint Council on Economic Education, 39

K
Kentucky, 28

L
Labor Unions, 31
Lancaster County Historical Society, Pennsylvania, 59
Landisville Camp Meeting Grounds, Pennsylvania, 62
Las Vegas, Nevada, 30
Le Sueur County Historical Society, Minnesota, 59

INDEX

Lubbock, Texas, 60, 64, 65

M
Mapping, 13, 24, 27, 41
Marling, Karal Ann, 68
Maryland, 59
Maryland Historical Society, 59
Massachusetts, 30, 37, 45
Mendocino County, California, 68
Mennonite, 62
Mershon Center, 28
Mesabi Iron Range, Minnesota, 44
Microfinance (Cambridge, MA), 30
Mid-American Program for Global Perspectives in Education, 28
Milwaukee, Wisconsin, employers, 34
Minneapolis, Minnesota Public Schools, 33
Minnehaha Falls, Minnesota, 58
Minnesota, 28, 31, 43–45, 58, 59, 65, 82
Minnesota and National Assessment of Educational Progress, 45
Moran, Thomas (American artist), 58
Motivation, student, 3
Museums as teaching aids, 37

N
National Council for the Social Studies, 2, 78
New Mexico, 28
New Ulm, Minnesota, 45
Niagara Falls, 58

O
Ohio, 28
Oklahoma, 28, 66
Old Sturbridge Village, Massachusetts, 37, 61
OPEC, 20, 22
Oregon, 44
Organization of Petroleum Exporting Countries, 47

P
Part-time employment, 3, 30–31
Peale Museum, Baltimore, Maryland, 59
Pennsylvania, 59, 60–62
Philbrook Art Center, Tulsa, Oklahoma, 66
Pomo Indians, 68
"Poppin' Fresh Pie Shops" (case study), 33
Preoccupations of youth, 1
Primary grades, 1, 78, 80

R
Ranching Heritage Center, Lubbock, Texas, 60

Reasoning, formal, 3
Revere, Paul, 59
Rochester, Minnesota, 31, 44, 82
Rocky Mountains, 58
Rotenberg, Jonathan, 30

S
San Antonio, Texas, 60
Santee Dacotah people, 44, 45
Savannah, Georgia, 71
Schools, elementary, 3, 6
Schools, junior high, 3
Self, conception and awareness of, 46–51
Social studies, student rank of, 3
Source evaluation, 54–56
Speakers, guest, 6–8, 12
St. Anthony, Falls of, 58
St. Louis County Historical Society, Minnesota, 59
St. Paul, Minnesota, 44, 65
Stockton, California, 28

T
Teachers, social studies, 1
Television advertisements, 30
Test of Economic Literacy, 39
Texas, 60, 64, 65, 71
Tulsa, Oklahoma, 66
Twin Cities, Minnesota, 65

V
Vermont, 28
Virginia, 44
Visual acuity/perception, 57–58
Visual arts, 57–58
Vorst, Joseph P. (American artist), 67
Voter participation, 75

W
Walker, Minnesota, 68
Washington, DC, 71
Winona County Historical Society, Minnesota, 59
Wisconsin, 29, 34
Worcester, Massachusetts, 59
World community, concerns of, 15
World interdependence, 15
Wozniak, Steve, 30

Y
Yale University, 59
Yosemite, 58
"You Can Bank On It" (case study), 33
Youth, concerns of, as consumers, 1, 29–30